DEADLY DINOSAURS

DEADLY DINOSAURS

Rupert Matthews,
Steve Parker

Miles
KeLLY

First published in 2011 by Miles Kelly Publishing Ltd
Harding's Barn, Bardfield End Green, Thaxted, Essex, CM6 3PX, UK

2 4 6 8 10 9 7 5 3 1

Publishing Director Belinda Gallagher
Creative Director Jo Cowan
Editorial Assistant Lauren White
Cover Designer Simon Lee
Designers Jo Cowan, Sally Lace, Sophie Pelham
Additional Design Kayleigh Allen
Image Manager Liberty Newton
Production Manager Elizabeth Collins
Reprographics Stephan Davis, Jennifer Hunt, Ian Paulyn

ISBN 978-1-84810-466-2

Printed in China

British Library Cataloguing-in-Publication Data
A catalogue record for this book is available from the British Library

Made with paper from a sustainable forest

www.mileskelly.net   info@mileskelly.net

www.factsforprojects.com

Self-publish your
children's book

buddingpress.co.uk

CONTENTS

PREHISTORIC LIFE

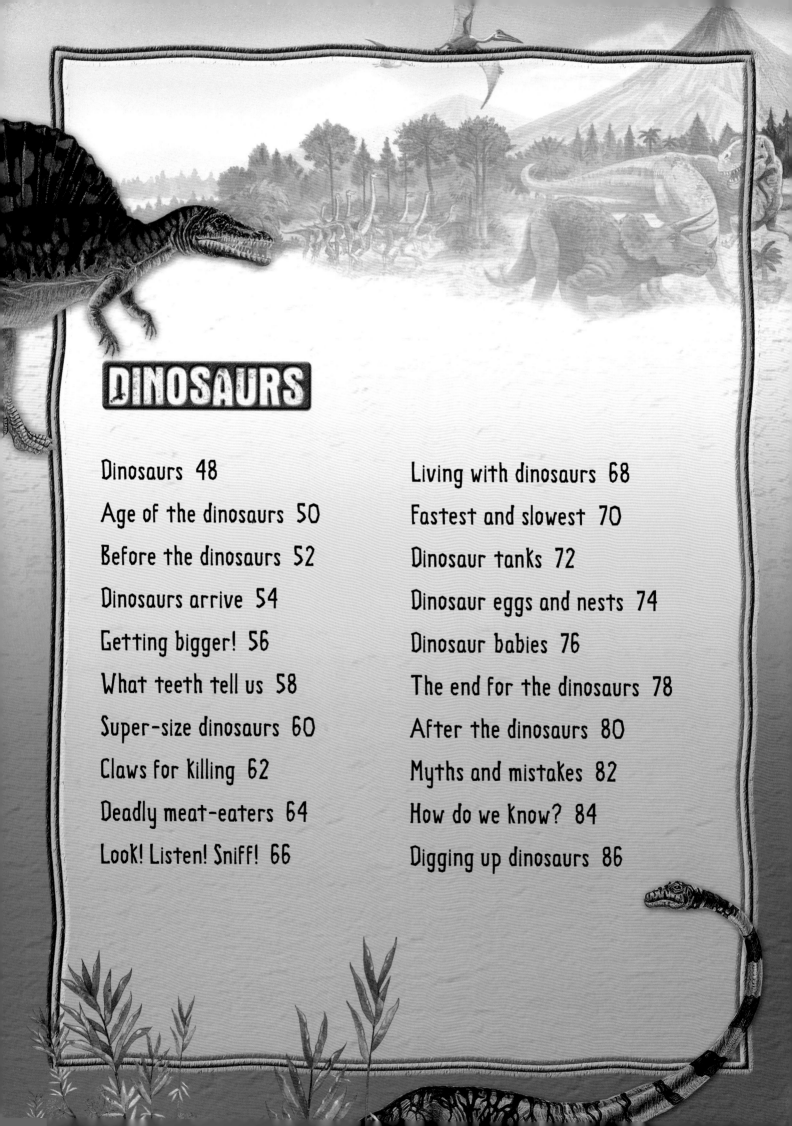

DINOSAURS

T REX

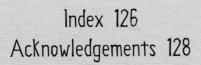

PREHISTORIC LIFE

The Earth was once covered by huge sheets of ice. This happened several times during Earth's history and we call these frozen times ice ages. However, the ice ages are a tiny part of prehistory. Before then, the world was warm and lakes and seas covered the land. Even earlier than this, there was little rain for thousands of years, and the land was covered in deserts. Over millions of years weather and conditions changed. Living things changed too, in order to survive. This change is called 'evolution'.

Woolly rhinoceros

Cave lion

▼ A scene from the last ice age, about 10,000 years ago. Animals grew thick fur coats to protect themselves from the cold. Many animals, such as woolly mammoths, survived on plants such as mosses. Others, such as cave lions, were fierce hunters, needing meat to survive.

Aurochs

Woolly mammoth

Megaloceros

Life begins

Life began a very, very long time ago. We know this from the remains of prehistoric life forms that died and were buried. Over millions of years, their remains turned into shapes in rocks, called fossils. The first fossils are over 3000 million years old. They are tiny 'blobs' called bacteria – living things that still survive today.

▼ Fossils of *Anomalocaris* have been found in Canada. It had a circular mouth and finlike body parts. Its body was covered by a shell.

The first plants were seaweeds, which appeared about 1000 million years ago. Unlike bacteria and blue-green algae, which each had just one living cell, these plants had thousands of cells. Some seaweeds were many metres long. They were called algae – the same name that scientists use today.

By about 800 million years ago, some plants were starting to grow on land. They were mixed with other living things called moulds, or fungi. Together, the algae (plants) and fungi formed flat green-and-yellow crusts that crept over rocks and soaked up rain. They were called lichens. These still grow on rocks and trees today.

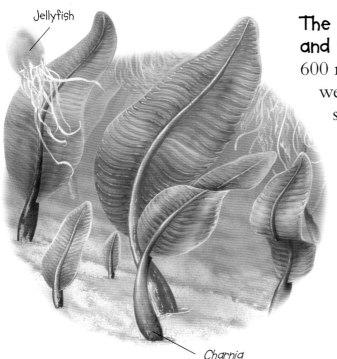

Jellyfish

Charnia

**The first animals lived in the sea –
and they were as soft as jelly!** Over
600 million years ago, some of the first animals
were jellyfish, floating in the water. On the
seabed lived groups of soft, feathery-
looking creatures called *Charnia*. This
animal was an early type of coral.
Animals need to take in food by eating
other living things. *Charnia* caught tiny
plants in its 'feathers'.

◄ *Charnia* looked like a prehistoric
plant, but it was actually an animal!

**One of the first hunting animals
was *Anomalocaris*.** It lived
520 million years ago, swimming
through the sea in search of prey. It
caught smaller creatures in its
pincers, then pushed them into
its mouth. *Anomalocaris* was a
cousin of crabs and insects.
It was one of the biggest
hunting animals of its time,
even though it was only
60 centimetres long.

▲ The *Cooksonia* plant had forked stems
that carried water. The earliest
examples have been found in Ireland.

**By 400 million years ago, plants on land were
growing taller.** They had stiff stems that held them
upright and carried water to their topmost parts. An
early upright plant was *Cooksonia*. It was the tallest
living thing on land, yet it was only 5 centimetres
high – hardly the size of your thumb!

Animals swarm the seas

Some of the first common animals were worms. However, they were not earthworms in soil. At the time there was no soil and the land was bare. These worms lived in the sea. They burrowed in mud for plants and animals to eat.

◄ *Ottoia* was a sea worm that fed by filtering tiny food particles from the sea.

▼ Trilobites moved quickly across the seabed. Some could roll up into a ball like woodlice do today. This was a means of protection.

The next animals to become common were trilobites. They first lived about 550 million years ago in the sea. Trilobites crawled along the seabed eating tiny bits of food they found. Their name means 'three lobes' (parts). A trilobite had two grooves along its back, from head to tail, so its body had three main parts – left, middle and centre.

▼ *Pterygotus* was a fierce hunter, with large eyes and long claws.

Trilobites were some of the first animals with legs that bent at the joints. Animals with jointed legs are called arthropods. They have been the most common creatures for millions of years, including trilobites long ago, and later on, crabs, spiders and insects. Like other arthropods, trilobites had a tough, outer shell for protection.

Some of the first hunters were sea scorpions – some were as big as lions! *Pterygotus* was 2 metres long. It swished its tail to chase prey through water, which it tore apart with its huge claws. Sea scorpions lived 500 to 250 million years ago. Unlike modern scorpions, they had no sting in their tails.

For millions of years the seabed was covered with the curly shells of **ammonites.** Some of these shells were as small as your fingernail, others were bigger than dinner plates. Ammonites were successful creatures and thousands of kinds survived for millions of years. Each ammonite had big eyes to see prey and long tentacles (arms) to catch it with. Ammonites died out at the same time as the dinosaurs, around 65 million years ago.

▲ This rock contains an ammonite fossil. The shell would have protected the soft-bodied creature inside.

◀ *Pikaia* looked a little bit like an eel with fins.

Among the worms, trilobites and ammonites was a small creature that had a very special body part – the beginnings of a backbone. It was called *Pikaia* and lived about 530 million years ago. Gradually, more animals with backbones, called vertebrates, evolved from it. Today, vertebrates rule much of the world – they are fish, reptiles, birds and mammals.

QUIZ

1. Did sea scorpions have stings in their tails?
2. What does the name 'trilobite' mean?
3. What kind of animal was *Ottoia*?
4. When did ammonites die out?
5. What was special about *Pikaia*?

Answers:
1. No 2. Three lobes, or parts 3. A worm 4. 65 million years ago 5. It had an early type of backbone

Very fishy

The first fish could not bite – they were suckers! About 500 million years ago, new animals appeared in the sea – the first fish. They had no jaws or teeth and probably sucked in worms and small pieces of food from the mud.

▲ *Hemicyclaspis* was an early jawless fish. It had eyes on top of its head and probably lived on the seabed. This way it could keep a look out for predators above.

Some early fish wore suits of armour! They had hard, curved plates of bone all over their bodies for protection. These fish were called placoderms and most were fierce hunters. Some had huge jaws with sharp sheets of bone for slicing up prey.

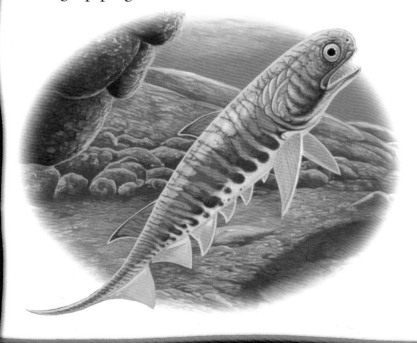

Spiny sharks had spines, but they were not really sharks. These fish were similar in shape to today's sharks, but they lived in rivers and lakes, not the sea, about 430 million years ago. *Climatius* was a spiny shark that looked fierce, but it was only as big as your finger!

◄ The fins on the back of *Climatius* were supported by needle-sharp spines. These helped to protect it from attacks by squid or other fish.

The first really big hunting fish was bigger than today's great white shark! *Dunkleosteus* grew to almost 10 metres in length and swam in the oceans 360 million years ago. It sliced up prey, such as other fish, using its massive teeth made of narrow blades of bone, each one as big as this book.

Some early fish started to 'walk' out of water. Types of fish called lobefins appeared 390 million years ago. Their side fins each had a 'stump' at the base made of muscle. If the water in their pool dried up, lobefins could use their fins like stubby legs to waddle over land to another pool. *Eusthenopteron* was a lobefin fish about one metre long. Over millions of years, some lobefins evolved into four-legged animals called tetrapods.

VERY FISHY!

You will need:
waxed card (like the kind used to make milk cartons) crayons scissors piece of soap

Place the piece of waxed card face down. Fold the card up at the edges. Draw a fish on the card. Cut a small notch in the rear of the card and wedge the piece of soap in it. Put the 'fish' in a bath of cold water and watch it swim away.

▼ *Eusthenopteron* could clamber about on dry land when moving from one stretch of water to another.

Animals invade the land

The first land animals lived about 450 million years ago. These early creatures, which came from the sea, were arthropods – creatures with hard outer body casings and jointed legs. They included prehistoric insects, spiders and millipedes. *Arthropleura* was a millipede – it was 2 metres in length!

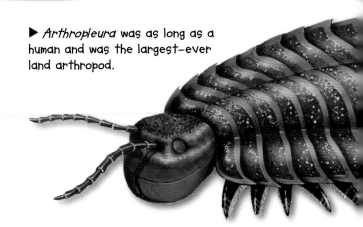

▶ *Arthropleura* was as long as a human and was the largest-ever land arthropod.

Some amphibians were fierce hunters. *Gerrothorax* was about one metre long and spent most of its time at the bottom of ponds or streams. Its eyes pointed upward, to see fish swimming past, just above. *Gerrothorax* would then jump up to grab the fish in its wide jaws.

The first four-legged animal had eight toes on each front foot! *Acanthostega* used its toes to grip water plants as it swam. It lived about 380 million years ago and was one metre long. Creatures like it soon began to walk on land, too. They were called tetrapods, which means 'four legs'. They were a big advance in evolution – the first land animals with backbones.

◀ *Acanthostega* probably spent most of its time in water. It had gills for breathing underwater as well as lungs for breathing air.

Soon four-legged animals called amphibians were racing across the land. Amphibians were the first backboned animals to move fast out of the water. *Aphaneramma* had long legs and could run quickly. However, prehistoric amphibians, like those of today such as frogs and newts, had to return to the water to lay their eggs.

Fins became legs for walking on land, and tails changed, too. As the fins of lobefin fish evolved into legs, their tails became longer and more muscular. *Ichthyostega* had a long tail with a fin along its upper side. This tail design was good for swimming in water, and also helpful when wriggling across a swamp.

Some amphibians grew as big as crocodiles! *Eogyrinus* was almost 5 metres long and had strong jaws and teeth, like a crocodile. However, it lived about 300 million years ago, long before any crocodiles appeared. Although *Eogyrinus* could walk on dry land, it spent most of its time in streams and swamps.

▼ *Ichthyostega* had short legs, so it could probably only move slowly on land.

Life after death

There were times in prehistory when almost everything died out. These times are called mass extinctions. Just a few types of plants and animals survive, which can then change, or evolve, into new kinds. A mass extinction about 290 million years ago allowed a fairly new group of animals to spread fast – the reptiles.

Reptiles' skin and eggs helped them to survive. Unlike an amphibian's, a reptile's scaly skin was waterproof. Also, the jelly-like eggs of amphibians had to be laid in water, while a reptile's eggs had tough shells for surviving on land. Around 280 million years ago, reptiles such as 1.5-metre-long *Varanosaurus* were spreading to dry areas where amphibians could not survive.

EDIBLE REPTILES

You will need:
100 grams dried milk   100 grams smooth peanut butter   2 tablespoons honey   currants   food colouring

Mix the dried milk, peanut butter and honey in a bowl. Mould this paste into reptile shapes. Decorate with currants for eyes and add food colouring for bright skin patterns. Then cause a mass extinction – eat them!

▲ *Varanosaurus* lived in what is now Texas, USA, and may have hunted fish in swamps.

▶ *Hylonomus* lived in forests in what is now Canada. It hunted insects, spiders and millipedes.

The first reptile looked like a lizard. However *Hylonomus* belonged to a different reptile group to lizards. It lived like a lizard, chasing prey on the ground and in trees. It lived 345 million years ago.

Some reptiles started to avoid bad weather by sleeping underground. *Diictodon* lived about 260 million years ago and used its large teeth to chop up tough plant food. It may have dug holes to shelter from the heat, cold and rain.

▼ *Diictodon* had strong legs and sharp claws for burrowing.

Wars around the world

Some amphibians fought back against the reptiles. *Mastodonsaurus* was a big, strong amphibian, 2 metres long, with sharp teeth. It hunted fish, other amphibians, and small reptiles. It lived at a time when reptiles were spreading even faster, about 250 to 203 million years ago. But most other big amphibians did not survive the reptiles.

▼ The nostrils and eyes of *Mastodonsaurus* were on top of its head so that it could breathe and look around whilst hiding underwater.

Other amphibians managed to survive the reptile takeover, too. They were mainly small and hid in water or swamps. One was *Branchiosaurus*, which was about 12 centimetres long and hunted small fish in ponds.

▲ *Lystrosaurus* lived in Antarctica when it was a land of lush, tropical plant life. Today it is a frozen continent, covered by thick ice.

I DON'T BELIEVE IT!

Mastodonsaurus may have had tusks sticking out of its nose! Two front teeth may have poked through holes at the end of its snout.

▼ As well as sharp teeth, *Moschops* had very strong skull bones, so it may have head-butted rivals in fights.

Reptiles showed how the world's lands moved about. *Lystrosaurus* lived about 200 million years ago and its fossils come from Europe, Asia, Africa and Antarctica. This reptile could not swim, so all of these landmasses, or continents, must have been joined together at one time. Over millions of years, they drifted apart to form today's positions.

Some plant-eating reptiles had very sharp teeth. *Moschops* was as big as a rhino and lived in southern Africa about 270 million years ago. Its teeth were long and straight, and ended with a sharp edge like a chisel. *Moschops* could easily bite tough leaves and twigs off bushes.

21

Reptiles take over

Reptiles don't like to be too hot, or too cold. Otherwise they may overheat, or be too cold to move. Most reptiles bask in sunshine to get warm, then stay in the shade. *Dimetrodon* was a fierce reptile. It had a large 'sail' of skin on its back to soak up heat from the sun.

▲ The name *Dimetrodon* means 'two-types-of-teeth'. It was given this name as it had stabbing teeth and slicing teeth. It measured 3 metres in length.

QUIZ

1. How did *Dimetrodon* get warm?
2. Which types of reptile evolved into mammals?
3. How did some early reptiles swim?
4. Did the first crocodiles like water?

Answers:
1. By basking in the sun
2. Therapsids 3. By swishing their tails from side to side 4. No, they hated it!

The first crocodiles hated water! An early type of crocodile, *Protosuchus*, stayed on land. It lived in North America about 190 million years ago. It was one metre long and could run across dry land when hunting, using its long legs.

▶ *Protosuchus* had very powerful jaw muscles to snap its teeth shut on prey.

▶ *Chasmatosaurus* had teeth on the roof of its mouth as well as in its jaws.

Some reptiles moved by using their tails. Many types of early reptiles had long, strong tails. They probably lived in water and swished their tails to push themselves along. *Chasmatosaurus* was 2 metres long and probably hunted for fish. It looked like a crocodile but was more closely related to the dinosaurs.

Some reptiles began to look very much like mammals. *Cynognathus* was as big as a large dog, and instead of scaly skin it had fur. It belonged to a group of reptiles called therapsids. Around 220 million years ago, some types of small therapsids were evolving into the first mammals.

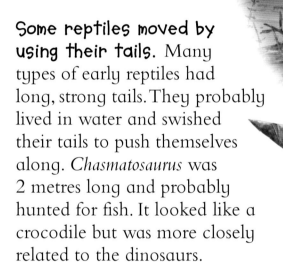

◀ The jaws of *Cynognathus* were so powerful they could bite through bone. Its name means 'dog jaw'.

Living with the dinosaurs

Some reptiles were as big and fierce as dinosaurs – but they lived in the sea. One of these was *Mosasaurus*. It grew up to 10 metres in length and may have weighed 10 tonnes, far bigger than today's great white shark.

One sea reptile had teeth the size of saucers! The huge, round, flat teeth of *Placodus* were more than 10 centimetres across. It used them to crush shellfish and sea urchins. *Placodus* was 2 metres long and lived at the same time as the first dinosaurs, about 230 million years ago.

I DON'T BELIEVE IT!

Fossils of Mosasaurus were found in the same place over 200 years apart! The first was found in a quarry in the Netherlands in 1780. The second was found in the same place in 1998.

▼ *Mosasaurus* was a huge sea reptile. It had razor-sharp teeth and could swim with speed to catch its prey.

▼ *Archaeopteryx* had a long bony tail, unlike modern birds, which have no bones in their tails.

Fossils of the first bird were mistaken for a dinosaur. *Archaeopteryx* lived in Europe about 155 million years ago. Some of its fossils look very similar to the fossils of small dinosaurs. So *Archaeopteryx* was thought to be a dinosaur, until scientists saw the faint shape of its feathers and realized it was a bird.

Soon there were many kinds of birds flying above the dinosaurs. *Confuciusornis* was about 60 centimetres long and lived in what is now China, 120 million years ago. It had a backwards-pointing big toe on each foot, which suggests it climbed through the trees. It is also the earliest-known bird to have a true beak.

▲ Fossils of *Confuciusornis* have been found in China. It is named after the famous Chinese wise man, Confucius.

Mammals lived at the same time as dinosaurs. These animals have warm blood, and fur or hair, unlike a reptile's scaly skin. *Megazostrodon* was the earliest mammal known to scientists. It lived in southern Africa about 215 million years ago — only 15 million years or so after the dinosaurs began life on Earth. It was just 12 centimetres long, and probably hunted insects.

▼ *Megazostrodon* probably came out at night to hunt for its insect prey. It looked a little like a modern-day shrew.

In and over the sea

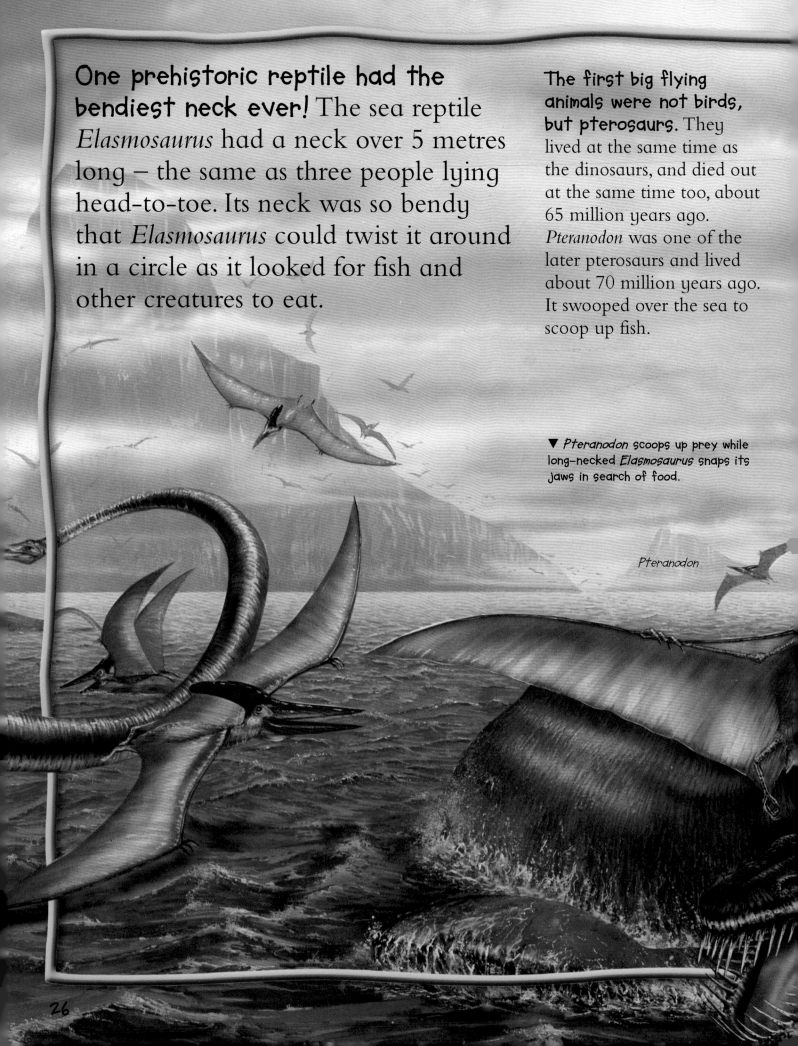

One prehistoric reptile had the bendiest neck ever! The sea reptile *Elasmosaurus* had a neck over 5 metres long – the same as three people lying head-to-toe. Its neck was so bendy that *Elasmosaurus* could twist it around in a circle as it looked for fish and other creatures to eat.

The first big flying animals were not birds, but pterosaurs. They lived at the same time as the dinosaurs, and died out at the same time too, about 65 million years ago. *Pteranodon* was one of the later pterosaurs and lived about 70 million years ago. It swooped over the sea to scoop up fish.

▼ *Pteranodon* scoops up prey while long-necked *Elasmosaurus* snaps its jaws in search of food.

Pteranodon

The largest flying animal of all time was as big as a plane! With wings measuring up to 14 metres from tip to tip, the pterosaur *Quetzalcoatlus* was twice as big as any flying bird. It may have lived like a vulture, soaring high in the sky, and then landing to peck at a dead body of a dinosaur.

Some fossils of sea creatures are found thousands of kilometres from the sea. Around 100 to 70 million years ago, much of what is now North America was flooded. The shallow waters teemed with all kinds of fish, reptiles and other creatures. Today their fossils are found on dry land.

Elasmosaurus

After the dinosaurs

A disaster about 65 million years ago killed off the dinosaurs and many other creatures. The main new group of animals was the mammals. Most were small, like rats and mice. *Leptictidium* lived 50 to 40 million years ago. It may be related to moles and shrews.

▲ *Leptictidium* probably hopped like a kangaroo!

Often the name of a prehistoric animal can be misleading, like *Palaeotherium*, which simply means 'ancient animal'. However this name was given over 200 years ago, in 1804, because scientists of the time did not know as much as modern scientists. Later studies show that *Palaeotherium* was one of the first animals in the group of hoofed mammals that includes horses.

◀ *Pakicetus* is the earliest-known whale.

Whales began life on dry land and gradually returned to the sea. *Pakicetus* lived about 50 million years ago and was nearly 2 metres long. It probably spent alot of time on land as well as in water.

▼ A mother *Uintatherium* and her baby. This strange-looking creature was the largest land animal of its time. Its head was covered in horns and it had small tusks.

Around 40 million years ago, the largest animal walking the Earth was *Uintatherium*. This plant eater was over 3 metres long and nearly 2 metres tall at the shoulder – about the same size as a cow. Its fossils were found near the Uinta River in Colorado, USA. *Uintatherium* is thought to be a cousin of horses and elephants.

An animal's looks can be misleading. *Patriofelis* means 'father of the cats'. It lived 45 million years ago and was named because scientists thought it was an early cat. Later they realized that it merely looked like a cat. It was really a member of an extinct group of hunting animals called creodonts.

QUIZ

1. What does the name *Patriofelis* mean?
2. How long was *Pakicetus*?
3. In what year were *Palaeotherium* fossils found?
4. How tall was *Uintatherium*?
5. When did dinosaurs die out and mammals start to take over?

Answers:
1. 'Father of the cats'
2. About 2 metres 3. 1804
4. Almost 2 metres tall at the shoulder
5. 65 million years ago

29

As the world cooled down

Before the world started to cool 30 million years ago, palm trees grew almost everywhere — but they became rare. These trees had thrived in warm, wet conditions. But as Earth cooled, other plants took over, such as magnolias, pines, oaks and birch. These changes meant that animals changed too.

▼ *Brontotherium* was somewhere in size between a rhino and an elephant. Males used the Y-shaped horn on their snouts in fighting competitions.

Pyrotherium means 'fire beast', but not because this plant eater could walk through fire. Its fossils were found in layers of ash from an ancient volcano in Argentina, South America. The volcano probably erupted, and its fumes and ash suffocated and burned all the animals nearby. *Pyrotherium* was about as big as a cow and looked like a combination of a pig and a short-tusked elephant.

Many prehistoric animals have exciting names — *Brontotherium* means 'thunder beast'. Where the fossils of *Brontotherium* were found in North America, local people thought they were bones of the gods. They thought that these gods rode chariots across the sky and started thunderstorms, which led to the animal's name.

Andrewsarchus was a real big-head!
At one metre long, it had the biggest
head of any hunting mammal on
land, and its strong jaws were filled
with sharp, pointed teeth. Its whole
body was bigger than a tiger of
today. *Andrewsarchus* probably lived
like a hyena, crunching up bones and
gristle from dead animals. Yet it
belonged to a mammal group that
was mostly plant eaters. It lived
30 million years ago in what is
now the deserts of Mongolia, Asia.

▲ *Andrewsarchus* was
the biggest meat-eating
land animal ever to
have lived.

QUIZ

1. What does
Brontotherium mean?
2. What does *Pyrotherium*
mean?
3. How long was the head
of *Andrewsarchus*?
4. Where did *Arsinoitherium*
live?

Answers:
1. 'Thunder beast' 2. 'Fire beast'
3. One metre 4. Northern Africa

▲ The horns on *Arsinoitherium's* head were hollow
and may have been used to make mating calls.

Some animals had horns as tall as
people! *Arsinoitherium's* two massive
horns looked like powerful weapons
– but they were light, fragile and
made of very thin bone. This plant
eater lived in northern Africa about
35 million years ago. It was almost
as big as an elephant and may have
been an ancient cousin of the
elephant group.

What fossils tell us

Fossils are the remains of animals or plants that have been preserved in rock. Usually only the hard parts of an animal, such as teeth or bones, are preserved in this way. Trilobites had a tough, outer skeleton so usually only this part of their body is found as a fossil. Scientists use the fossil to try to create a picture of how the soft parts, such as muscles and organs, may have looked.

▼ Some early humans are known only from their fossil footprints, not from fossils of their bones. These footprints were discovered in 1978 in Tanzania, Africa.

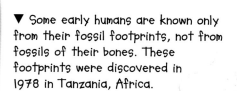

▲ By examining trilobite fossils, scientists were able to tell that this animal could see in all directions.

Some fossils are known as trace fossils. These are not fossilized parts of an animal's body, such as bones, but preserved marks left behind by the animal, such as footprints or droppings. By studying the fossilized footprints of an extinct animal, scientists can discover how it walked, how fast it could move and whether it lived alone or in groups.

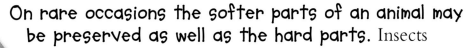

On rare occasions the softer parts of an animal may be preserved as well as the hard parts. Insects may become trapped in sticky sap oozing from pine trees. This sap may then become fossilized as amber, with the insect caught inside. Scientists have found hundreds of insects, spiders and other small creatures perfectly preserved in this way.

▲ Amber spider fossils show that spiders have changed little over the last 30 million years.

QUIZ

1. What is a fossil?
2. What could scientists tell from trilobite fossils?
3. What is amber?
4. What animals did *Archaeopteryx* look like?

Answers:
1. Remains of animals or plants preserved in rock 2. That they could see in all directions 3. Fossil tree sap 4. A bird and a dinosaur

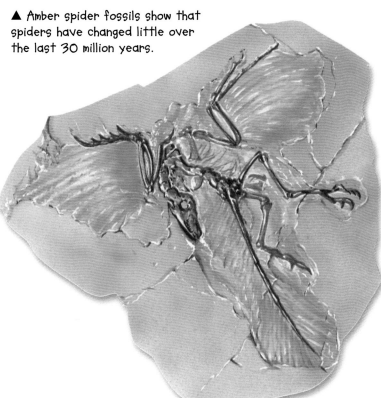

◀ Some fossils of *Archaeopteryx* are so well preserved that even the feathers can be seen.

One of the most important and valuable fossils ever found was of *Archaeopteryx*, in Germany in 1860. The fossil is about 150 million years old and shows a creature that looked part dinosaur and part bird. It had the feathers and wings of a bird, but the teeth and bony tail of a dinosaur. This shows that birds probably evolved from a type of dinosaur.

The importance of some fossils can be misunderstood. *Acanthostega* was one of the very earliest amphibian fossils ever found. However, the man who found the fossil was not an expert on amphibians. When his expedition returned from Greenland, the fossil was put in a drawer at a museum. It was not until over 30 years later that an expert on amphibians happened to see the fossil and realized how important it was.

Prehistoric prowlers

Some animals probably ate just about anything. Entelodonts were piglike animals that lived about 25 million years ago. *Dinohyus* was one of the largest entelodonts. Its teeth were sharp and strong, and it had powerful jaw muscles. It ate almost anything from leaves, roots and seeds, to small animals.

Some predators (hunting animals) walked on tiptoe but others were flat-footed. Most mammal predators, such as cats and dogs, walk on the ends of their toes. This helps them to run faster. *Daphoenodon* walked on flat feet, like a bear. It is often called a 'bear-dog' as it looked like a dog but walked like a bear.

▼ *Dinohyus* lived in North America and grew to be about 3 metres long. Its powerful neck muscles and large canine teeth suggest it could have broken bones and eaten flesh.

Fossils can show if predators hunted by day or at night. *Plesictis* was 75 centimetres long and its fossils show it had large sockets (spaces) for its eyes. This means that it probably hunted at night. It also had sharp claws and a long tail, so it probably scampered through trees hunting birds and insects, gripping with its claws and balancing with its tail.

Some predators have changed little over millions of years. *Potamotherium* was an early otter and lived in Europe, 23 million years ago. It looked almost like the otters of today. Its shape was so well-suited to hunting fish in streams that it has hardly changed.

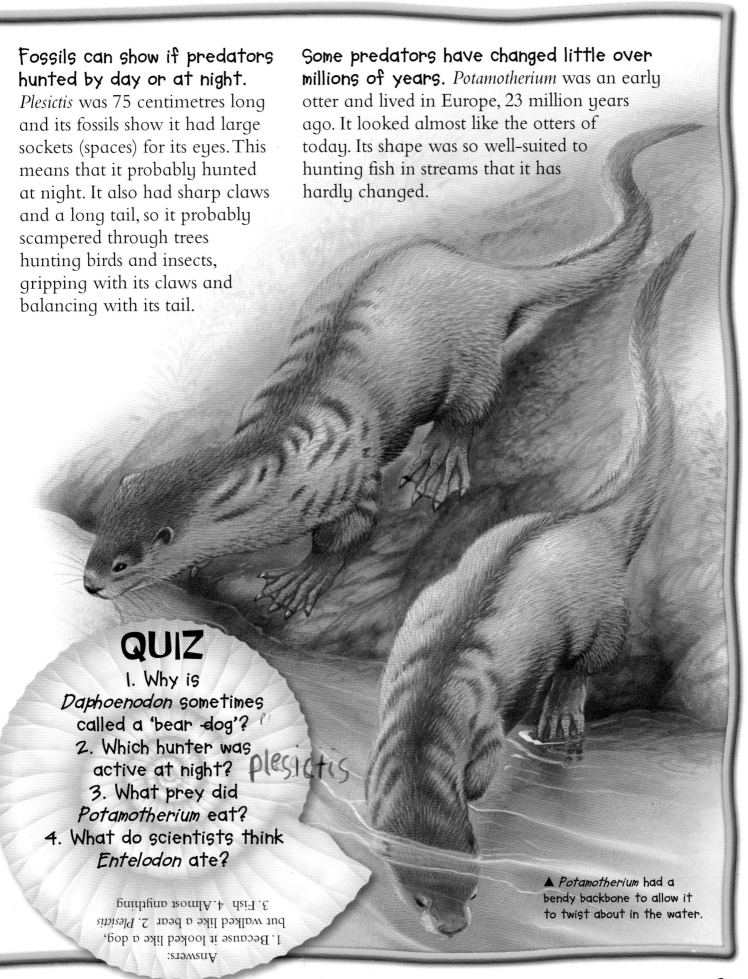

plesictis

▲ *Potamotherium* had a bendy backbone to allow it to twist about in the water.

QUIZ
1. Why is *Daphoenodon* sometimes called a 'bear-dog'?
2. Which hunter was active at night?
3. What prey did *Potamotherium* eat?
4. What do scientists think *Entelodon* ate?

Answers:
1. Because it looked like a dog, but walked like a bear 2. *Plesictis*
3. Fish 4. Almost anything

Amazing ancient elephants

The first elephant had tiny tusks and almost no trunk. *Moeritherium* lived in northern Africa about 36 million years ago. It stood just 60 centimetres tall and may have weighed around 20 kilograms – about the size of a large pet dog.

I DON'T BELIEVE IT!

The tusks of *Anancus* were over 4 metres long – almost as long as the animal itself.

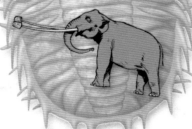

▶ Woolly mammoths had coats of shaggy hair. This hair kept their warm inner fur dry and waterproof in the freezing conditions of the ice age.

Some elephants were very hairy. The woolly mammoth was covered in thick, long dense hair to keep out the cold of the ice age. It was larger than a modern elephant and was probably hunted by early people. The last woolly mammoths may have died out less than 10,000 years ago.

One elephant had tusks like shovels. *Platybelodon* lived about nine million years ago in Europe, Asia and Africa. Its lower tusks were shaped like broad, flat shovels. Perhaps it used them to scoop up water plants to eat.

Some elephants had four tusks. *Tetralophodon* lived about eight million years ago and stood 3 metres tall. Its fossils have been found in Europe, Asia, Africa and America, so it was a very widespread and successful animal.

The biggest elephant was the Columbian mammoth. It stood 4 metres tall and may have weighed over 10 tonnes – twice as much as most elephants today. It lived on the grasslands of southern North America.

▼ The Columbian mammoth had tusks that twisted into curved, spiral shapes.

Elephants were more varied and common long ago, than they are today. *Anancus* roamed Europe and Asia two million years ago. Like modern elephants, it used its trunk to pull leaves from branches and its tusks to dig up roots. However most kinds of prehistoric elephants died out. Only two kinds survive today, in Africa and Asia.

Animals with hooves

The first horse was hardly larger than a pet cat. *Hyracotherium* lived in Europe, Asia and North America about 50 million years ago. It was only 20 centimetres tall and lived in woods and forests.

▲ *Hyracotherium* is sometimes called *Eohippus*, which means 'dawn horse'. It had a short neck, slender legs and a long tail.

Early horses did not eat grass — because there wasn't any. Grasses and open plains did not appear on Earth until 25 million years ago. Then early horses moved onto them, started to eat grass, and gradually became bigger.

Over millions of years, horses gradually lost their toes! The very first horses had five toes per foot, each ending in a small nail-like hoof. *Hyracotherium* had four toes on each front foot and three on each back foot. Later, *Mesohippus*, which was as big as a labrador dog, had three toes on each foot. Today's horses have just one toe on each foot, which ends in a large hoof.

Some prehistoric camels had horns. *Synthetoceras* had a pair of horns at the top of its head, and also an extraordinary Y-shaped horn growing from its nose. It probably used these horns to fight enemies and also to show off to others of its kind at breeding time.

▶ The amazing nose horn of *Synthetoceras* was present only on male animals.

HORSE RACE

You will need:
stiff card crayons
scissors string
about 4 metres long

On the card, draw a picture of *Hyracotherium*. Colour it in and cut it out. Make a hole in the middle, about 2 centimetres from the top. Thread the string through the hole and tie one end to a piece of furniture. Pull the string tight, then flick it with a finger to make *Hyracotherium* move along!

◀ *Megaloceros* may have stored food for the winter in the form of fat in a hump on its shoulder.

Some prehistoric deer had antlers as big as a person! *Megaloceros* means 'big deer' and it was as big as today's biggest deer, the moose. But its antlers were even bigger, measuring almost 4 metres from tip to tip. *Megaloceros* may have survived in some parts of Europe until as little as 3000 years ago.

Cats, dogs and bears

The sabre-tooth 'tiger' *Smilodon* had two huge sharp teeth like sabres (swords) — but it was not really a tiger. It belonged to a different group of cats to real tigers. *Smilodon*'s teeth were long and sharp but not very strong. It probably used them like knives to stab and slash at its prey, which then bled to death. *Smilodon* then ate it without a struggle.

▶ *Smilodon* had enormously powerful shoulders, so it may have sprung on its prey and held it down.

The earliest cats were similar to those of today. *Dinictis* lived about 30 million years ago and was strong and stealthy, like the modern-day cougar (mountain lion). It probably hunted like modern cats too, by creeping up close to a victim, then leaping on it to bite its throat or neck.

The first dog, *Hesperocyon*, had a long body and short legs, more like a stoat or mongoose. It was about 90 centimetres long and lived about 30 million years ago. Only later dogs had long legs and were able to run fast after their prey.

◀ *Hesperocyon* may have hunted in packs. This would have allowed it to hunt animals much larger than itself.

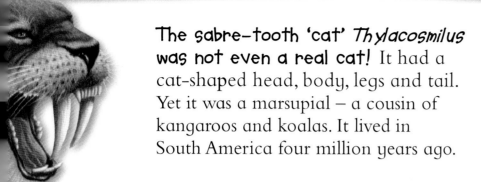

The sabre-tooth 'cat' *Thylacosmilus* was not even a real cat! It had a cat-shaped head, body, legs and tail. Yet it was a marsupial – a cousin of kangaroos and koalas. It lived in South America four million years ago.

Sea lions did not develop from lions – but from dogs. *Allodesmus* was an early type of sea lion and lived about 13 million years ago. It had strong flippers for fast swimming. Its fossil bones show that it came originally from the dog group.

I DON'T BELIEVE IT!
Even if global warming continues, the world will not be as hot as it was 35 million years ago.

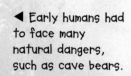
◀ Early humans had to face many natural dangers, such as cave bears.

Early people hunted cave bears, and cave bears hunted early people! The huge cave bear of the Ice Age was as big as today's grizzly bear. Humans called Neanderthals hunted them and used their bones and teeth as ornaments. The bears hunted people too, and left their bones in caves.

Prehistoric giants

The largest flying bird ever was as big as a small plane! *Argentavis* was twice the size of any flying bird today. Its wings measured 7 metres from tip to tip. It was a huge vulture that fed on the dead bodies of other creatures, tearing off their flesh with its powerful hooked beak.

▼ *Argentavis* lived about seven million years ago in South America.

Some birds were even bigger than *Argentavis*, **but they could not fly – and they were deadly hunters.** In South America about one million years ago, *Titanis* grew to 3 metres tall. It raced after its prey, which it tore apart with its huge, hooked beak.

▶ in South America, *Titanis* was a monstrous hunting bird that chased after mammals such as this early horse.

A type of prehistoric kangaroo, *Procoptodon*, **was twice as big as those of today.** Yet it could bound along as fast as a racehorse. Like kangaroos of today, it was a marsupial, carrying its baby in a pouch. It lived in Australia.

The largest land mammal ever to have lived was a type of rhino – without a nose horn. *Paraceratherium* was far bigger than an elephant, at 8 metres long and 6 metres tall at the shoulder. It weighed over 15 tonnes – more than three elephants. This giant creature lived in Asia about 30 million years ago and was a peaceful plant eater.

I DON'T BELIEVE IT!
Giant marsupials may have started stories of the 'Bunyip', a mythical Australian animal.

▲ The huge *Paraceratherium* fed by browsing on trees, stripping off the leaves. Even though it was so big and heavy, *Paraceratherium* had long legs, which means it was probably capable of running.

A giant island

For almost 50 million years, South America was like a giant island – with many strange animals that were found nowhere else. Until three million years ago, South America was separated from North America by an ocean. On islands, animals can evolve into unusual kinds found nowhere else in the world.

▶ South America was once separated from North America. This meant that certain animals that survived there, such as *Macrauchenia* and *Glyptodon*, did not live anywhere else in the world.

Elephants were not the only animals with trunks! *Macrauchenia* lived in South America about 100,000 years ago. It was about the size of a camel and probably had a trunk to gather leaves to eat. It was not a type of elephant, but a distant cousin of horses and rhinos.

Armadillos were once nearly as big as tanks! *Glyptodon* was almost 4 metres long and covered in a thick dome of bony armour. It lived in South America until about 10,000 years ago. Today, armadillos are quite small, but they are still covered in bony plates for protection.

Macrauchenia

Glyptodon

One South American creature that has died out was the giant sloth, *Megatherium*. It was a cousin of the smaller sloths that live in trees today – but it was far too big to climb trees. At 6 metres long and 3 tonnes in weight, it was the size of an elephant!

When South America joined North America, many kinds of prehistoric animals died out. In particular, animals from North America spread south. They were better at surviving than the South American creatures, and they gradually took over.

▶ *Megatherium* may only have died out in the last few thousand years.

I DON'T BELIEVE IT!
The armadillo is a South American animal that lives in North America, too. Over the past 100 years, it has spread north at a rate of one kilometre every ten years.

Our prehistoric relations

Monkeys, apes and humans first appeared over 50 million years ago – the first kinds looked like squirrels. This group is called the primates. *Plesiadapis* was one of the first primates. It lived 55 million years ago in Europe and North America.

◄ *Plesiadapis* had claws on its fingers and toes, unlike monkeys and apes, which had nails.

I DON'T BELIEVE IT

The first fossils of the giant ape *Gigantopithecus* to be studied by scientists came from a second-hand shop in Hong Kong, over 70 years ago.

Early apes walked on all fours. About 20 million years ago, *Dryopithecus* lived in Europe and Asia. It used its arms and legs to climb trees. When it came down to the ground, it walked on all fours. It was 60 centimetres long and ate fruit and leaves.

► The early ape *Dryopithecus* walked flat on its feet, unlike other apes, which walked on their knuckles.

▼ The need to see longer distances on grasslands may have caused the first apes to walk on two legs.

Some kinds of apes may have walked on their two back legs, like us. About 4.5 million years ago *Ardipithecus* lived in Africa. Only a few of its fossils have been found. However, experts think it may have walked upright on its back legs. It could have made the first steps in the change, or evolution, from apes to humans.

One prehistoric ape was a real giant – it was more than 3 metres tall! Its name, *Gigantopithecus*, means 'giant ape'. It was much larger than today's biggest ape, the gorilla, which grows up to 2 metres tall. *Gigantopithecus* probably ate roots and seeds, and may have hunted small animals such as birds, rats and lizards.

▶ The enormous *Gigantopithecus* could probably stand on its hind legs to reach food.

Scientists work out which animals are our closest cousins partly from fossils – and also from chemicals. The chemical called DNA contains genes, which are instructions for how living things grow and work. The living animals with DNA most similar to ours are the great apes, chimpanzees and gorillas, both from Africa. So our ancient cousins were probably apes like them. The orang-utan, from Southeast Asia, is less similar.

DINOSAURS

Dinosaurs were types of animals with scaly skin, called reptiles. They lived millions of years ago. There were many different kinds of dinosaurs - huge and tiny, tall and short, fierce hunters and peaceful plant-eaters. But all the dinosaurs died out long, long ago.

Age of the dinosaurs

Dinosaurs lived between about 230 million and 65 million years ago. This vast length of time is called the Mesozoic Era. Dinosaurs were around for about 80 times longer than people have been on Earth!

Dinosaurs were not the only animals during the Mesozoic Era. There were many other kinds of animals such as insects, fish, lizards, crocodiles, birds and mammals.

There were many different shapes and sizes of dinosaurs. Some were smaller than your hand. Others were bigger than a house!

▼ *Jobaria* and *Janenschia*, giant plant eaters.

▼ This timeline begins 286 million years ago at the start of the Permian Period when the ancestors of the dinosaurs appear. It finishes at the end of the Tertiary Period 2 million years ago, when the dinosaurs die out and mammals became dominant.

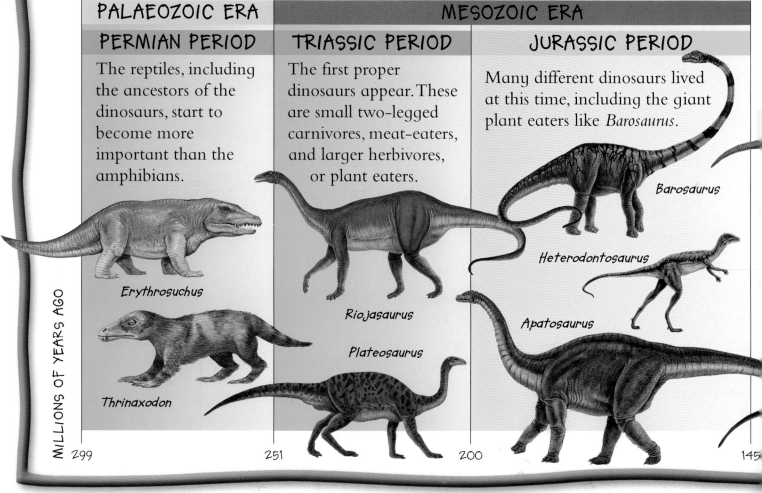

PALAEOZOIC ERA	MESOZOIC ERA	
PERMIAN PERIOD	TRIASSIC PERIOD	JURASSIC PERIOD
The reptiles, including the ancestors of the dinosaurs, start to become more important than the amphibians.	The first proper dinosaurs appear. These are small two-legged carnivores, meat-eaters, and larger herbivores, or plant eaters.	Many different dinosaurs lived at this time, including the giant plant eaters like *Barosaurus*.

Erythrosuchus

Thrinaxodon

Riojasaurus

Plateosaurus

Barosaurus

Heterodontosaurus

Apatosaurus

MILLIONS OF YEARS AGO

299   251   200   145

No single kind of dinosaur survived for all of the Mesozoic Era. Different dinosurs came and went. Some lasted for less than a million years. Other kinds, like *Stegosaurus*, kept going for more than 20 million years.

There were no people during the Age of Dinosaurs. There was a gap of more than 60 million years between the last dinosaurs and the first people.

I DON'T BELIEVE IT!

The name 'dinosaur' means 'terrible lizard'. But dinosaurs weren't lizards, and not all dinosaurs were terrible. Small plant-eating dinosaurs were about as 'terrible' as today's sheep!

◄ All the dinosaurs died out at the end of the Cretaceous Period, possibly because of a meteor strike, but no one can be sure.

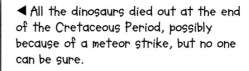

MESOZOIC ERA	CENOZOIC ERA
CRETACEOUS PERIOD	TERTIARY PERIOD

During the last part of the age of the dinosaurs, both giant carnivores and armoured herbivores were alive.

The dinosaurs have all died out. Mammals, which have been around since the Triassic Period, become the main land animals.

Tyrannosaurus rex

Deinonychus

Brontotherium, herbivorous mammal

Spinosaurus

Thylacosmilus, carnivorous mammal

Nesodon, herbivorous mammal

Tarbosaurus

145

66

2

MILLIONS OF YEARS AGO

Before the dinosaurs

Dinosaurs were not the first animals on Earth. Many other kinds of creatures lived before them, including several other types of reptiles. Over millions of years one of these groups of reptiles probably changed very slowly, or evolved, into the first dinosaurs.

Therapsids lived before the dinosaurs and also alongside the early dinosaurs. They were called mammal-like reptiles because they didn't have scaly skin like most reptiles. They had furry or hairy skin like mammals.

▲ *Dimetrodon* was 3 metres long and had a tall flap of skin like a sail on its back.

Dimetrodon was a fierce, meat-eating reptile that looked like a dinosaur — but it wasn't. It lived 270 million years ago, long before the dinosaurs.

Crocodiles were around even before the first dinosaurs. They still survive today, long after the last dinosaurs. *Erythrosuchus* was 4.5 metres long, lived 240 million years ago, lurked in swamps and ate fish.

Thecodonts were slim, long- legged reptiles that lived just before the dinosaurs. They could rear up and run fast on their back legs. They could also leap and jump well. They probably caught small animals such as bugs and lizards to eat.

◄ *Erythrosuchus* was a crocodile-like reptile that lived long before the dinosaurs.

Of all the creatures shown here, the thecodonts were most similar to the first dinosaurs. So perhaps some thecodonts gradually changed, or evolved, into early dinosaurs. This may have happened more than 220 million years ago. But no one is sure, and there are many other ideas about where the dinosaurs came from.

▼ *Ornithosuchus* was one of the early thecodonts. It was a carnivore that walked on two legs, a cousin of the first dinosaurs. The name 'thecodont' means 'socket-toothed reptile'.

Dinosaurs arrive

The earliest dinosaurs stalked the Earth almost 230 million years ago. They lived in what is now Argentina, in South America. They included *Eoraptor* and *Herrerasaurus*. Slim and fast creatures, they could stand almost upright and run on their two rear legs. Few other animals of the time could run upright like this, on legs that were straight below their bodies. Most other animals had legs that stuck out sideways.

Herrerasaurus was about 3 metres long from nose to tail.

The legs were underneath the body, not sticking out to the sides as in other reptiles, such as lizards and crocodiles.

These early dinosaurs were probably meat eaters. They hunted small reptiles such as lizards, insects and worms. They had lightweight bodies and long, strong legs to chase after prey. Their claws were long and sharp for grabbing victims. Their large mouths were filled with pointed teeth to tear up their food.

TWO LEGS GOOD!
You will need:

stiff card   sticky tape
safe scissors   split pins

Cut out a model of *Herrerasaurus*; the head, body, arms and tail are one piece of card. Next, cut out each leg from another piece. Fix the legs on either side of the hip area of the body using a split pin. Adjust the angle of the head, body and tail to stand over the legs. This is how many dinosaurs stood and ran, well balanced over their rear legs and using little effort.

Herrerasaurus had a pointed head and a long, bendy neck, which helped it to look around and sniff for prey.

The long tail balanced the head and body over the rear legs.

Herrerasaurus could run rapidly on its two rear legs, or walk slowly on all fours.

Getting bigger!

As the early dinosaurs spread over the land they began to change. This gradual and natural change in living things has happened since life began on Earth. New kinds of plants and animals appear, do well for a time, and then die out as yet more new kinds appear. The slow and gradual change of living things over time is called evolution.

Plateosaurus

Some kinds of dinosaurs became larger and began to eat plants rather than animals. *Plateosaurus* was one of the first big plant-eating dinosaurs. It grew up to 8 metres long and lived 220 million years ago in what is now Europe. It could rear up on its back legs and use its long neck to reach food high off the ground.

Riojasaurus was an even larger plant eater. It lived 218 million years ago in what is now Argentina. *Riojasaurus* was 10 metres long and weighed about 2 tonnes - more than a large family car of today.

Riojasaurus

The early dinosaurs lived during the Triassic Period. This was the first period or part of the Age of Dinosaurs (the Mesozoic Era). The Triassic Period lasted from 251 to 200 million years ago.

The early plant-eating dinosaurs may have become larger so that they could reach up into trees for food. Their size would also have helped them fight enemies, as many big meat-eating reptiles were ready to make a meal of them. One was the crocodile *Rutiodon* which was 3 metres long.

▼ *Rutiodon*, a crocodile-like meat eater, waits for *Riojasaurus*. It may be thinking about dinner!

I DON'T BELIEVE IT!

Early plant-eating dinosaurs did not eat fruits or grasses — there weren't any! They hadn't appeared yet! Instead they ate plants called horsetails, ferns, cycads, and conifer trees.

What teeth tell us

We know about living things from long ago, such as dinosaurs, because of fossils. These were once their hard body parts, such as bones, claws, horns and shells. The hard parts did not rot away after death but got buried and preserved for millions of years. Gradually they turned to stone and became fossils. Today, we dig up the fossils, and their sizes and shapes give us clues to how prehistoric animals lived.

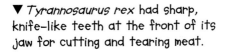

▼ Plant eater *Edmontosaurus* had flat teeth at the back of its jaws for chewing its food.

▼ *Tyrannosaurus rex* had sharp, knife-like teeth at the front of its jaw for cutting and tearing meat.

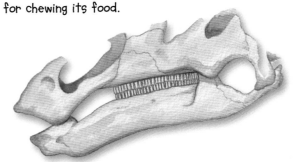

Dinosaur teeth were very hard and formed many fossils. Their shapes help to show what each type of dinosaur ate. Edmontosaurus had rows of broad, wide, sharp-ridged teeth in the sides of its mouth. These were ideal for chewing tough plant foods like twigs and old leaves.

▶ *Tarbosaurus* was 12 metres long and lived 70 million years ago in East Asia.

Tarbosaurus had long, sharp teeth like knives or daggers. These were excellent for tearing up victims, and slicing off lumps of flesh for swallowing.

▼ *Baryonyx* was 10 metres long and lived 120 million years ago in Europe.

Baryonyx had small, narrow, pointed, cone-shaped teeth. These resemble the teeth of a crocodile or dolphin today. They are ideal for grabbing slippery prey such as fish.

The teeth of the giant, long-necked dinosaur *Apatosaurus* were long, thin and blunt, shaped like pencils. They worked like a rake to pull leaves off branches into the mouth, for the dinosaur to eat.

▶ *Apatosaurus* was 25 metres long and lived 140 million years ago in Western North America.

FIND DINOSAUR TEETH AT HOME!

With the help of an adult, look in a utensils drawer or tool box for dinosaur teeth! Some tools resemble the teeth of some dinosaurs, and do similar jobs.
File or rasp – broad surface with hard ridges, like the plant-chewing teeth of *Edmontosaurus*.
Knife – long, pointed and sharp, like the meat-slicing teeth of *Tyrannosaurus rex*.
Pliers – Gripping and squeezing, like the beak-shaped mouth of *Ornithomimus*.

▲ *Ornithomimus* was 3.5 metres long and lived 70 million years ago in western North America.

Some dinosaurs, like *Ornithomimus*, had no teeth at all! The mouth was shaped like a bird's beak and made out of a tough, strong, horny substance like our fingernails. The beak was suited to pecking up all kinds of food such as seeds, worms and bugs.

Super-size dinosaurs

The true giants of the Age of Dinosaurs were the sauropods. These vast dinosaurs all had a small head, long neck, barrel-shaped body, long tapering tail and four pillar-like legs. The biggest sauropods included *Brachiosaurus*, *Mamenchisaurus*, *Barosaurus*, *Diplodocus* and *Argentinosaurus*.

▲ *Argentinosaurus* was up to 40 metres long, and weighed up to 100 tonnes.

Sauropod dinosaurs probably lived in groups or herds. We know this from their footprints, which have been preserved as fossils. Each foot left a print as large as a chair seat. Hundreds of footprints together shows that many sauropods walked along in groups.

Sauropod dinosaurs may have swallowed pebbles – on purpose! Their peg-like teeth could only rake in plant food, not chew it. Pebbles and stones gulped into the stomach helped to grind and crush the food. These pebbles, smooth and polished by the grinding, have been found with the fossil bones of sauropods.

The biggest sauropods like *Apatosaurus* were enormous beasts. They weighed up to ten times more than elephants of today. Yet their fossil footprints showed they could run quite fast – nearly as quickly as you!

Mamenchisaurus grew up to 26 metres long and weighed 30 tonnes. It lived in East Asia 160 million years ago.

Barosaurus lived 150 million years ago in North America and Africa. It was 27 metres long and weighed 15 tonnes.

Brachiosaurus grew up to 25 metres long, and weighed up to 50 tonnes. It lived 150 million years ago in North America and Africa.

Diplodocus lived in North America 150 million years ago. It grew to 27 metres long and weighed up to 12 tonnes.

Sauropods probably had to eat most of the time, 20 hours out of every 24. They had enormous bodies that needed great amounts of food, but only small mouths to gather the food.

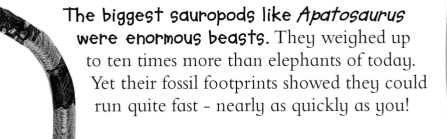

This modern lorry is to the same scale as these huge dinosaurs!

I DON'T BELIEVE IT!

Diplodocus is also known as 'Old Whip-tail'! It could swish its long tail so hard and fast that it made an enormous CRACK like a whip. This living, leathery, scaly whip would scare away enemies or even rip off their skin.

Claws for Killing

Nearly all dinosaurs had claws on their fingers and toes. These claws were shaped for different jobs in different dinosaurs. They were made from a tough substance called keratin – the same as your fingernails and toenails.

Hypsilophodon

Hypsilophodon had strong, sturdy claws. This small plant eater, 2 metres long, probably used them to scrabble and dig in soil for seeds and roots.

Deinonychus had long, sharp, hooked claws on its hands. This meat eater, about 3 metres long, would grab a victim and tear at its skin and flesh.

Deinonychus

Deinonychus also had a huge hooked claw, as big as your hand, on the second toe of each foot. This claw could kick out and flick down like a pointed knife to slash pieces out of the prey.

Baryonyx also had a large claw but this was on the thumb of each hand. It may have worked as a fish-hook to snatch fish from water. This is another clue that *Baryonyx* probably ate fish.

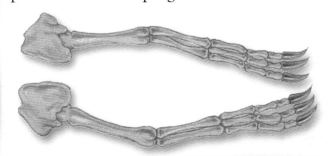

◀ These giant arms of the dinosaur *Deinocheirus* were found in Mongolia. Each one was bigger than a human, but nothing else of the skeleton has yet been found.

Iguanodon had claws on its feet.
But these were rounded
and blunt and looked
more like hooves.

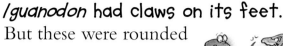

Iguanodon

Iguanodon also had stubby claws on its hands. However its thumb claw was longer and shaped like a spike, perhaps for stabbing enemies.

QUIZ

Compare these modern animals' claws to the dinosaurs and their claws shown here. Which modern animal has claws with a similar shape and job to each dinosaur?

1. Lion — sharp, tearing claws

2. Deer — Rounded blunt hooves

3. Elephant — Flat, nail-like claws

4. Mole — Broad, strong digging claws

Answers:
1. *Deinonychus* 2. *Iguanodon*
3. *Apatosaurus* 4. *Hypsilophodon*

Giant sauropod dinosaurs had almost flat claws. Dinosaurs like *Apatosaurus* looked like they had toenails on their huge feet!

Deadly meat-eaters

The biggest meat-eating dinosaurs were the largest predators (hunters) ever to walk the Earth. Different types came and went during the Age of Dinosaurs. *Allosaurus* was from the middle of this time span. One of the last dinosaurs was also one of the largest predators – *Tyrannosaurus rex*. An earlier hunting dinosaur from South America was even bigger – *Giganotosaurus*.

▼ *Tyrannosaurus rex* may have hunted for prey in small groups.

Meat-eating dinosaurs probably caught their food in various ways. They may have lurked behind rocks or trees and rushed out to surprise a victim. They may have raced as fast as possible after prey that ran away or plodded steadily for a great time to tire out their meal. They might even have scavenged – feasted on the bodies of creatures which were dead or dying.

I DON'T BELIEVE IT!

Some meat-eating dinosaurs not only bit their prey, but also each other! Fossils of several *Tyrannosaurus rex* had bite marks on the head. Perhaps they fought each other to become chief in the group, like wolves today.

These great predators were well equipped for hunting large prey – including other dinosaurs. They all had massive mouths armed with long sharp teeth in powerful jaws. They had long, strong back legs for fast running, and enormous toe claws for kicking and holding down victims.

Carnotaurus from South America was 7.5 metres long and weighed one tonne

Allosaurus was 11 metres long and weighed 2 tonnes. It came from North America

The famous *Tyrannosaurus rex* was 13 metres long and weighed 5 tonnes. It lived in North America.

The biggest carnivore was *Giganotosaurus*. It was over 13 metres long and weighed over 6 tonnes

Spinosaurus came from Africa. It was 14 metres long and weighed 4 tonnes

Albertosaurus was from North America. It was 9 metres long and weighed one tonne

Look! Listen! Sniff!

Like the reptiles of today, dinosaurs could see, hear and smell the world around them. We know this from fossils. The preserved fossil skulls have spaces for eyes, ears and nostrils.

Some dinosaurs like *Troodon* had very big eyes. There are large, bowl-shaped hollows in their fossil skulls. Today's animals with big eyes can see well in the dark, like mice, owls and night-time lizards. Perhaps *Troodon* prowled through the forest at night, peering in the gloom for small creatures to eat.

▶ *Troodon* was about 2 metres long and lived in North America 70 million years ago.

There are also spaces on the sides of the head where *Troodon* had its ears. Dinosaur ears were round and flat, like the ears of other reptiles. *Troodon* could hear the tiny noises of little animals moving about in the dark.

Ear

Eye

Nostril

Troodon skull

The nostrils of *Troodon*, where it breathed in air and smelled scents, were two holes at the front of its snout. With its delicate sense of smell, *Troodon* could sniff out its prey of insects, worms, little reptiles such as lizards, and small shrew-like mammals.

Dinosaurs used their eyes, ears and noses not only to find food, but also to detect enemies – and each other. *Parasaurolophus* had a long, hollow, tube-like crest on its head. Perhaps it blew air along this to make a noise like a trumpet, as an elephant does today with its trunk.

Dinosaurs like *Parasaurolophus* may have made noises to send messages to other members of their group or herd. Different messages could tell the others about finding food or warn them about enemies.

BIGGER EYES, BETTER SIGHT

Make a *Troodon* mask from card. Carefully cut out the shape as shown. Carefully cut out two small eye holes, each just one cm across. Attach elastic so you can wear the mask and find out how little you can see. Carefully make the eye holes as large as the eyes of the real *Troodon*. Now you can have a much bigger, clearer view of the world!

▼ *Parasaurolophus* was a 'duck-billed' dinosaur or hadrosaur. It was about 10 metres long and lived 80 million years ago in North America.

Living with dinosaurs

All dinosaurs walked and ran on land, as far as we know. No dinosaurs could fly in the air or spend their lives swimming in the water. But many other creatures, which lived at the same time as the dinosaurs, could fly or swim. Some were reptiles, like the dinosaurs.

Ichthyosaurs were reptiles that lived in the sea. They were shaped like dolphins, long and slim with fins and a tail. They chased after fish to eat.

Plesiosaurs were also reptiles that swam in the sea. They had long necks, tubby bodies, four large flippers and a short tail.

Turtles were another kind of reptile that swam in the sea during the Age of Dinosaurs. Each had a strong, domed shell and four flippers. Turtles still survive today, but ichthyosaurs and plesiosaurs died out with the dinosaurs, long ago.

Turtle

Plesiosaur

Ichthyosaur

▼ Hadrosaurs like *Anatosaurus* were duck-billed dinosaurs with a long, wide tail like a crocodile's tail. Perhaps *Anatosaurus* swished this from side to side to swim now and again. But it did not live in the water.

◄ Predators like *Velociraptor* were meat-eating dinosaurs with large arms, wrists and hands. Over millions of years these could have evolved feathers to become a bird's wings.

Birds first appeared about 150 million years ago. It is possible that over millions of years certain small, meat-eating dinosaurs called raptors developed feathers. Slowly their arms became wings. Gradually they evolved into the very first birds.

Birds evolved after the dinosaurs, but birds did overlap with the dinosaurs. Some dived for fish in the sea, very much like birds such as gulls and terns today.

Ichthyornis

Pterosaurs were reptiles that could fly. They had thin, skin-like wings held out by long finger bones. Some soared over the sea and grabbed small fish in their sharp-toothed, beak-shaped mouths. Others swooped on small land animals.

Rhamphorynchus

QUIZ

Which of these are NOT dinosaurs?

A Pterosaur

B Raptor

C Plesiosaur

D Hadrosaur

E Ichthyosaur

F Bird

Answer:
A Pterosaur, C Pleasiosaur,
E Icthyosaur, F Bird

Fastest and slowest

Dinosaurs walked and ran at different speeds, according to their size and shape. In the world today, cheetahs and ostriches are slim with long legs and run very fast. Elephants and hippos are massive heavyweights and plod slowly. Dinosaurs were similar. Some were big, heavy and slow. Others were slim, light and speedy.

▼ *Coelophysis* was 3 metres long. It was one of the earliest dinosaurs, living about 220 million years ago.

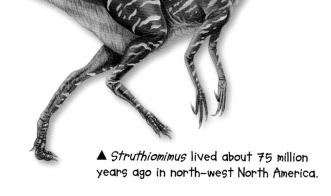

▲ *Struthiomimus* lived about 75 million years ago in north-west North America.

Struthiomimus was one of the fastest of all the dinosaurs. It was more than 2 metres tall and 4 metres long. It had very long back legs and large clawed feet, like an ostrich. It also had a horny beak-shaped mouth for pecking food, like an ostrich. This is why it is also called an 'ostrich-dinosaur'. It could probably run at more than 70 kilometres per hour.

Muttaburrasaurus was a huge ornithopod type of dinosaur, a cousin of *Iguanodon*. It probably walked about as fast as you, around 4–5 kilometres per hour. It might have been able to gallop along at a top speed of 15 kilometres per hour, making the ground shake with its 4-tonne weight!

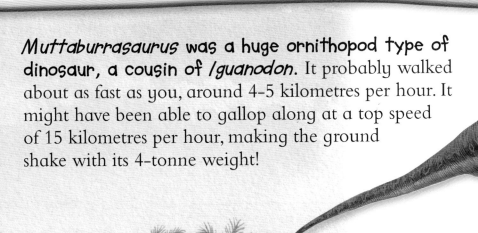

▲ *Muttaburrasaurus* lived about 110 million years ago in south-east Australia.

Coelophysis was a slim, lightweight dinosaur. It could probably trot, jump, leap and dart about with great agility. Sometimes it ran upright on its two back legs. Or it could bound along on all fours like a dog at more than 30 kilometres per hour.

QUIZ

Put these dinosaurs and today's animals in order of top running speed, from slowest to fastest.

Human (40 km/h)

Cheetah (100-plus km/h)

Struthiomimus (70 km/h)

Muttaburrasaurus (15 km/h)

Sloth (0.2 km/h)

Coelophysis (30 km/h)

Answer:
Sloth, Muttaburrasaurus,
Coelophysis, Human, Struthiomimus,
Cheetah

Dinosaur tanks

Some dinosaurs had body defences against predators. These might be large horns and spikes, or thick hard lumps of bonelike armour-plating. Most armoured dinosaurs were plant eaters. They had to defend themselves against big meat-eating dinosaurs such as *Tyrannosaurus rex*.

Triceratops had three horns, one on its nose and two much longer ones above its eyes. It also had a wide shield-like piece of bone over its neck and shoulders. The horns and neck frill made *Triceratops* look very fearsome. But most of the time it quietly ate plants. If it was attacked, *Triceratops* could charge at the enemy and jab with its horns, like a rhino does today.

▲ *Triceratops* was 9 metres long and weighed over 5 tonnes. It lived 65 million years ago in North America.

Euoplocephalus **was a well-armoured dinosaur.** It had bands of thick, leathery skin across its back. Big, hard, pointed lumps of bone were set into this skin like studs on a leather belt. *Euoplocephalus* also had a great lump of bone on its tail. It measured almost one metre across and looked like a massive hammer or club. *Euoplocephalus* could swing it at predators to injure them or break their legs.

DESIGN A DINOSAUR!

Make an imaginary dinosaur! It might have the body armour and tail club of *Euoplocephalus*, or the head horns and neck frill of *Triceratops*.
You can draw your dinosaur, or make it out of pieces of card or from modelling clay. You can give it a made-up name, like Euoplo-ceratops or Tri-cephalus. How well protected is your dinosaur? How does it compare to some well-armoured creatures of today, such as a tortoise, armadillo or porcupine?

Styracosaurus

Protoceratops

Euoplocephalus

Dinosaur eggs and nests

Like most reptiles today, dinosaurs produced young by laying eggs. These hatched out into baby dinosaurs, which gradually grew into adults. Fossils have been found of eggs with developing dinosaurs inside, as well as fossils of just-hatched baby dinosaurs.

Many kinds of dinosaur eggs have been found. *Protoceratops* was a pig-sized dinosaur that lived 85 million years ago in what is now the Gobi Desert of Asia.

◄ A fossilized baby dinosaur inside an egg.

A *Protoceratops* female arranged her eggs. The eggs were carefully positioned in a spiral shape, or in circles one within the other.

▼ A female *Protoceratops* with her eggs.

Protoceratops scraped a bowl-shaped nest about one metre across in the dry soil. Probably the female did this. Today, only female reptiles make nests and some care for the eggs or babies. Male reptiles take no part.

Protoceratops' egg

The eggs probably hatched after a few weeks. The eggshell was slightly leathery and bendy, like most reptile eggshells today, and not brittle or hard like a bird's.

▶ This shows part of a *Tyrannosaurus rex* egg.

Fossils of baby *Protoceratops* show that they looked very much like their parents. But the neck frill of the baby *Protoceratops* was not as large compared to the rest of the body, as in the adult. As the youngster grew, the frill grew faster than the rest of the body.

QUIZ

1. How long was *Triceratops*?
2. How many horns did *Triceratops* have?
3. How many eggs did a female *Protoceratops* lay?
4. Did dinosaurs lay hard eggs like birds, or bendy eggs?
5. How long was a *Tyrannosaurus rex* egg?

Answers:
1. 9 metres 2. Three
3. About 20 eggs 4. They laid bendy, leathery eggs 5. 40 centimetres

Other dinosaurs laid different sizes and shapes of eggs. Huge sauropods like *Brachiosaurus* probably laid rounded eggs as big as basketballs. Eggs of big meat eaters such as *Tyrannosaurus rex* were more sausage-shaped, 40 centimetres long and 15 centimetres wide.

Most dinosaurs simply laid their eggs in a nest or buried in soil, and left them to hatch on their own. The baby dinosaurs had to find their own food and defend themselves against enemies. But other dinosaurs looked after their babies.

Dinosaur babies

Some dinosaur parents looked after their babies and even brought them food in the nest. Fossils of the hadrosaur dinosaur *Maiasaura* include nests, eggs, babies after hatching, and broken eggshells. Some fossils are of unhatched eggs but broken into many small parts, as though squashed by the babies which had already come out of their eggs.

The newly hatched *Maiasaura* babies had to stay in the nest. They could not run away because their leg bones had not yet become strong and hard. The nest was a mound of mud about 2 metres across, and up to 20 babies lived in it.

▶ Hundreds of fossil *Maiasaura* nests have been found close together, showing that these dinosaurs bred in groups or colonies. The nests show signs of being dug out and repaired year after year, which suggests the dinosaurs kept coming back to the same place to breed.

Fossils of *Maiasaura* nests also contain fossilised twigs, berries and other bits of plants. *Maiasaura* was a plant-eating dinosaur, and it seems that one or both parents brought food to the nest for their babies to eat. The tiny teeth of the babies already had slight scratches and other marks where they had been worn while eating food. This supports the idea that parent *Maiasaura* brought food to their babies in the nest.

I DON'T BELIEVE IT!

Baby dinosaurs grew up to five times faster than human babies! A baby sauropod dinosaur like *Diplodocus* was already one metre long and 30 kilograms in weight when it came out of its egg!

The end for the dinosaurs

All dinosaurs on Earth died out by 65 million years ago. There are dinosaur fossils in the rocks up to this time, but there are none after. However, there are fossils of other creatures like fish, insects, birds and mammals. What happened to wipe out some of the biggest, most numerous and most successful animals the world has ever seen? There are many ideas. It could have been one disaster, or a combination of several.

The dinosaurs may have been killed by a giant lump of rock, a meteorite. This would have come from outer space and smashed into the Earth. A meteorite would have thrown up vast clouds of water, rocks, ash and dust that blotted out the Sun for many years. Lack of sunlight would mean that plants could not grow so plant-eating dinosaurs died out. Meat-eating dinosaurs had no food so they died as well.

Dinosaurs might have been killed by a disease. This could have gradually spread among all the dinosaurs and killed them off.

It might be that dinosaur eggs were eaten by a plague of animals. Small, shrew-like mammals were around at the time. They may have eaten the eggs at night as the dinosaurs slept.

Many volcanoes around the Earth could have erupted all at the same time. This would have thrown out red-hot rocks, ash, dust and clouds of poison gas. Dinosaurs would have choked and died in the gloom.

▼ A giant meteorite from space may have killed off not only the dinosaurs, but many other kinds of animals and plants too.

METEORITE SMASH!

You will need:

plastic bowl   flour
large pebble   desk light

Ask an adult for help. Put the flour in the bowl. This is Earth's surface. Place the desk light so it shines over the top of the bowl. This is the Sun. The pebble is the meteorite from space. WHAM! Drop the pebble into the bowl. See how the tiny bits of flour float in the air like a mist, making the 'Sun' dimmer. A real meteorite smash may have been the beginning of the end for the dinosaurs.

79

After the dinosaurs

From 65 million years ago there were no dinosaurs left. Dinosaurs were not the only group of animals to perish at that time. The flying reptiles called pterosaurs and the swimming reptiles, ichthyosaurs and plesiosaurs, also died. When a group of living things dies out completely, this is known as extinction. When many groups of living things all disappear at about the same time, this is a mass extinction.

▼ *Diatryma*, a giant flightless bird

Even though many kinds of animals and plants died out 65 million years ago, many other groups lived on. Insects, worms, fish, birds and mammals all survived the mass extinction – and these groups are still alive today.

Even though the dinosaurs and many other reptiles died out in the mass extinction, several groups of reptiles did not. Crocodiles, turtles and tortoises, lizards and snakes all survived. Why some kinds of reptiles like dinosaurs died out in the mass extinction, yet other types did not still puzzles dinosaur experts today.

Hesperocyon   *Hyracotherium*

▼ The mass extinction of 65 million years ago killed the dinosaurs and many other kinds of animals and plants. But plenty of animals survived, such as mammals and birds.

After the mass extinction, two main groups of animals began to take the place of the dinosaurs and spread over the land. These were birds and mammals. No longer were mammals small and skulking, coming out only after dark when the dinosaurs were asleep. The mammals changed or evolved to become bigger, with many kinds – from peaceful plant eaters to huge, fierce predators.

I DON'T BELIEVE IT!

The earliest birds had wings and flapped through the skies. But many of the birds that appeared after the dinosaurs could not fly!

Myths and mistakes

As far as we can tell from the clues we have, some of the ideas which have grown up about dinosaurs are not true. For example, dinosaurs are shown in different colours such as brown or green. Some have patches or stripes. But no one knows the true colours of dinosaurs. There are a few fossils of dinosaur skin. But being fossils, these have turned to stone and so they are the colour of stone. They are no longer the colour of the original dinosaur skin.

▼ We really have no idea what colour the dinosaurs were. We can guess by looking at reptiles today, but they could have been any colour!

◄ This is a fossil of the skin of *Edmontosaurus*. You can see the texture of the skin, but the only colour is of the rock.

▲ *Troodon* had a large brain for its body size, almost the same as a monkey of today.

Similarly, for many years people thought that all dinosaurs were slow and stupid animals. But they were not. Some dinosaurs were quick and agile. Also some, like *Troodon*, had big brains for their body size. They may have been quite 'clever'.

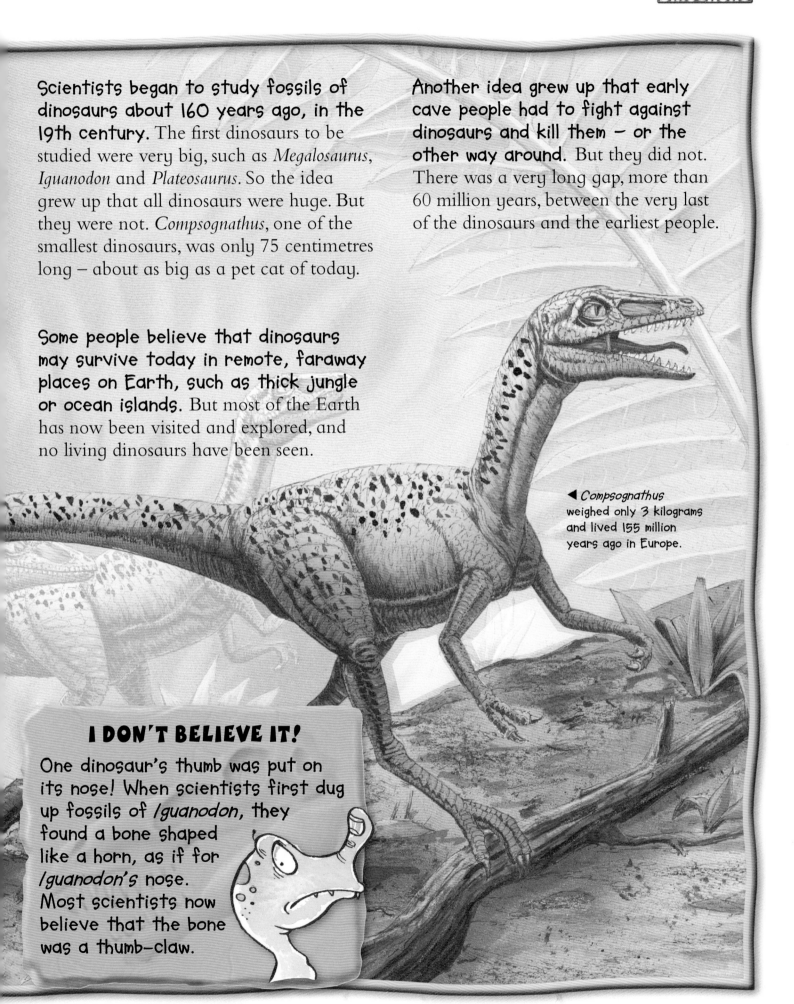

Scientists began to study fossils of dinosaurs about 160 years ago, in the 19th century. The first dinosaurs to be studied were very big, such as *Megalosaurus*, *Iguanodon* and *Plateosaurus*. So the idea grew up that all dinosaurs were huge. But they were not. *Compsognathus*, one of the smallest dinosaurs, was only 75 centimetres long – about as big as a pet cat of today.

Some people believe that dinosaurs may survive today in remote, faraway places on Earth, such as thick jungle or ocean islands. But most of the Earth has now been visited and explored, and no living dinosaurs have been seen.

Another idea grew up that early cave people had to fight against dinosaurs and kill them – or the other way around. But they did not. There was a very long gap, more than 60 million years, between the very last of the dinosaurs and the earliest people.

◄ *Compsognathus* weighed only 3 kilograms and lived 155 million years ago in Europe.

I DON'T BELIEVE IT!

One dinosaur's thumb was put on its nose! When scientists first dug up fossils of *Iguanodon*, they found a bone shaped like a horn, as if for *Iguanodon's* nose. Most scientists now believe that the bone was a thumb-claw.

How do we Know?

▼ All living things die. Those living in water, such as this ichthyosaur, are more likely to leave fossils than those on land.

We know about dinosaurs mainly from their fossils. Fossils took thousands or millions of years to form. Most fossils form on the bottoms of lakes, rivers or seas, where sand and mud can quickly cover them over and begin to preserve them. If the animal is on dry land, they are more likely to be eaten, or simply to rot away to nothing.

Very rarely, a dinosaur or other living thing was buried soon after it died. Then a few of the softer body parts also became fossils, such as bits of skin or the remains of the last meal in the stomach.

1. After death, the ichthyosaur sinks to the seabed. Worms, crabs and other scavengers eat its soft body parts.

The body parts most likely to fossilize were the hardest ones, which rot away most slowly after death. These included animal parts such as bones, teeth, horns, claws and shells, and plant parts such as bark, seeds and cones.

Not all dinosaur fossils are from the actual bodies of dinosaurs. Some are the signs, traces or remains that they left while alive. These include eggshells, nests, tunnels, footprints, and claw and teeth marks on food.

Dinosaur droppings also formed fossils! They have broken bits of food inside, showing what the dinosaur ate. Some dinosaur droppings are as big as a TV set!

QUIZ

Which body parts of a dinosaur were most likely to become fossils? Remember, fossils form from the hardest, toughest bits that last long enough to become buried in the rocks and turned to stone.

Skull bone	Blood
Muscle	Claws
Leg bone	Eye
Scaly skin	Teeth

Answer:
Skull bone, leg bone, teeth and claws were most likely to form fossils

2. Sediments cover the hard body parts, such as bones and teeth, which gradually turn into solid rock.

3. Millions of years later the upper rock layers wear away and the fossil remains are exposed.

Digging up dinosaurs

Every year, thousands of dinosaur fossils are discovered. Most of them are from dinosaurs already known to scientists. But five or ten might be from new kinds of dinosaurs. From the fossils, scientists try to work out what the dinosaur looked like and how it lived, all those millions of years ago.

Most dinosaur fossils are found by hard work. Fossil experts called palaeontologists study the rocks in a region and decide where fossils are most likely to occur. They spend weeks chipping and digging the rock. They look closely at every tiny piece to see if it is part of a fossil. However some dinosaur fossils are found by luck. People out walking in the countryside come across a fossil tooth or bone by chance. What a discovery!

Finding all the fossils of a single dinosaur, neatly in position as in life, is very rare indeed. Usually only a few fossil parts are found from each dinosaur. These are nearly always jumbled up and broken.

▼ These are palaeontologists, scientists that look for and study dinosaur bones, uncovering a new skeleton.

People dig carefully into the rock with hammers, picks and brushes.

Scientists make notes, sketches and photographs, to record every stage of the fossil 'dig'.

Cleaning fossils

Laying out fossils

The fossils are taken back to the palaeontology laboratory. They are cleaned and laid out to see which parts are which. It is like trying to put together a jigsaw, with most of the pieces missing. Even those which remain are bent and torn. The fossils are put back together, then soft body parts that did not form fossils, such as skin, are added. Scientists use clues from similar animals alive today, such as crocodiles, to help 'rebuild' the dinosaur.

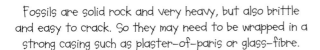

▲ A rebuilt skeleton is displayed in a museum.

Fossils are solid rock and very heavy, but also brittle and easy to crack. So they may need to be wrapped in a strong casing such as plaster-of-paris or glass-fibre.

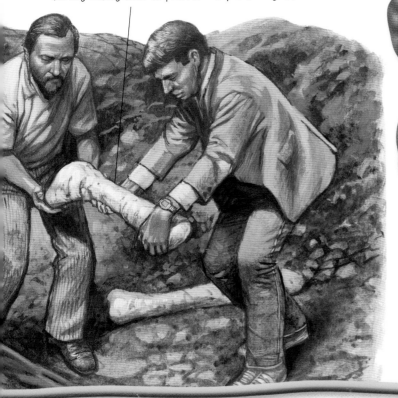

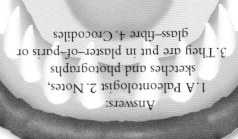

QUIZ

1. What do we call a scientist that studies fossils?

2. How is a fossil 'dig' recorded?

3. How are fossils packed to protect them?

4. What animals can scientists compare dinosaurs fossils with?

Answers:
1. A Palaeontologist 2. Notes, sketches and photographs 3. They are put in plaster-of-paris or glass-fibre 4. Crocodiles

Almost everyone has heard of *Tyrannosaurus rex*. Wasn't it the biggest dinosaur of all time, the greatest meat eater with a mouth big enough to swallow a car and teeth as long as swords? Not one of these 'facts' is true. Certainly *Tyrannosaurus rex* is one of the world's most famous animals. Even though it died out 65 million years ago, it 'lives on' in movies, toys and games, as statues and works of art, and in music and songs. However, *Tyrannosaurus rex* is also the subject of many mistaken beliefs.

▶ A scene from the 2005 movie *King Kong*. With a mighty roar *Tyrannosaurus rex* bares its huge mouth filled with sharp teeth and prepares to attack. Images like this are familiar — but are they correct? For example, did *T rex* really roar loudly?

Terror of its age

▲ The last dinosaurs of the Late Cretaceous Period ranged from small, speedy hunters such as *Avimimus* to giant plant eaters, three-horned *Triceratops*, spiky *Edmontonia*, hadrosaurs or 'duckbilled' dinosaurs with strange head crests, and of course *T rex*.

KEY

1 *Tyrannosaurus rex*	5 *Parasaurolophus*	9 *Struthiomimus*
2 *Triceratops*	6 *Lambeosaurus*	10 *Albertosaurus*
3 *Stegoceras*	7 *Avimimus*	11 *Therizinosaurus*
4 *Edmontonia*	8 *Corythosaurus*	12 *Euoplocephalus*

T rex's full name is *Tyrannosaurus rex*, which means 'king of the tyrant lizards'. However, it wasn't a lizard. It was a large carnivorous or meat-eating animal in the reptile group known as the dinosaurs.

Dinosaurs, or 'terrible lizards', lived during a time called the Mesozoic Era (251–65 million years ago). The first dinosaurs appeared about 230 million years ago and all had died out, or become extinct, by 65 million years ago.

There were hundreds of kinds of dinosaurs. *Plateosaurus* was a bus-sized herbivore (plant eater) from 210 million years ago. *Brachiosaurus* was a giant herbivore from 150 million years ago. *Deinonychus* was a fierce hunter from about 110 million years ago, and was about the size of an adult human.

QUIZ

Which of these extinct animals were dinosaurs?

Pterodactyl
Tyrannosaurus rex
Woolly mammoth
Archaeopteryx   Triceratops
Plateosaurus   Ammonite

Answer:
*Tyrannosaurus rex,
Triceratops, Plateosaurus*

Tyrannosaurus rex lived well after all of these dinosaurs. Its time was the last part of the Mesozoic Era, known as the Cretaceous Period (145–65 million years ago), from about 68 to 65 million years ago. *T rex* was one of the very last dinosaurs.

ERA	PERIOD	MYA (Million years ago)
MESOZOIC	CRETACEOUS 145–65 MYA	— 70 — 80 — 90 — 100 — 110 — 120 — 130 — 140
	JURASSIC 200–145 MYA	— 150 — 160 — 170 — 180 — 190 — 200
	TRIASSIC 251–200 MYA	— 210 — 220 — 230 — 240 — 250

Jurassic Period: *Allosaurus* was a big meat-eating dinosaur

Triassic Period: *Herrerasaurus* was one of the first dinosaurs

◀ Dinosaurs ruled the land for 160 million years — longer than any other animal group.

A giant predator

The size of big, fierce animals such as great white sharks, tigers and crocodiles can be exaggerated (made bigger). People often think *T rex* was bigger than it really was.

A full-grown T rex was over 12 metres long and more than 3 metres high at the hips. It could rear up and raise its head to more than 5 metres above the ground.

▼ *Tyrannosaurus rex* may have been big, but it was smaller than all the other creatures shown here.

Brachiosaurus
13 metres tall
25 metres nose to tail
40–plus tonnes in weight

Tyrannosaurus rex was not such a giant compared to some plant-eating animals. It was about the same weight as today's African bush elephant, half the size of the extinct imperial mammoth, and one-tenth as heavy as some of the biggest plant-eating dinosaurs.

Imperial mammoth
4.5 metres tall
12 metres nose to tail
10 tonnes in weight

T rex
3–4 metres tall
11–12 metres nose to tail
5 tonnes in weight

Sperm whale
20 metres nose to tail
50 tonnes in weight

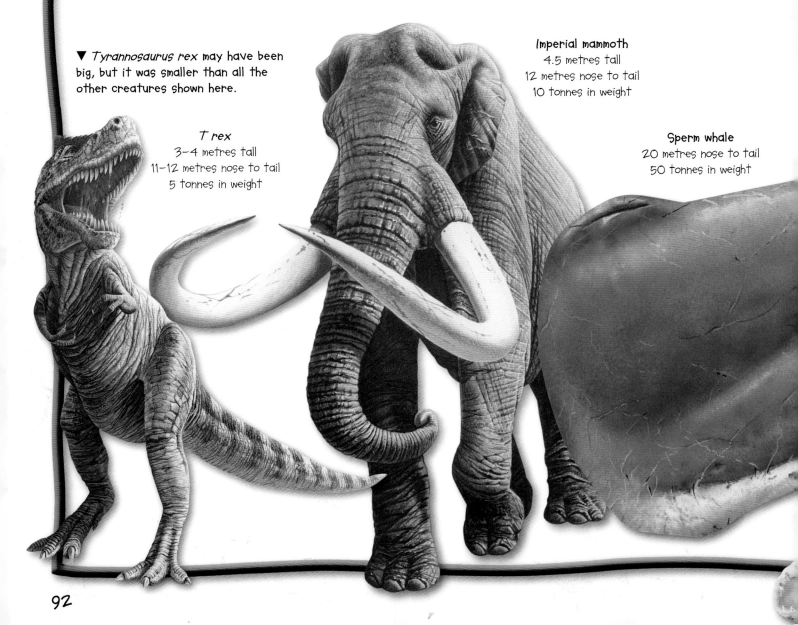

Compared to today's biggest meat-eating land animals, *Tyrannosaurus rex* was huge. The largest land carnivores today are polar and grizzly bears, up to 3 metres tall and over 600 kilograms. However that's only one-tenth of the weight of *T rex*.

Compared to other extinct meat eaters, *Tyrannosaurus rex* was large. The wolf-like *Andrewsarchus* from 40 million years ago was one of the biggest mammal land carnivores. It stood 2 metres tall, was 4 metres long from nose to tail, and weighed more than one tonne.

Tyrannosaurus rex is sometimes called 'the biggest predator of all time'. However it was only one-tenth the size of the sperm whale living in today's oceans, which hunts giant squid. It was also smaller than prehistoric ocean predators such as the pliosaurs *Liopleurodon* and *Kronosaurus* (10 tonnes or more) and the ichthyosaur *Shonisaurus* (more than 20 tonnes).

Compare huge hunters

You will need:
pens   large sheet of paper   animal books

In books or on the Internet, find side-on pictures of *T rex*, a sperm whale, a killer whale and *Andrewsarchus*. Draw them on one sheet of paper to see how they compare:
Sperm whale as long as the paper
T rex nose to tail two-thirds as long as the sperm whale
Killer whale half as long as the sperm whale
Andrewsarchus one-fifth as long as the sperm whale

Profile of T rex

Fossil experts can work out what an extinct animal such a *Tyrannosaurus rex* looked like when it was alive. They study the size, shape, length, thickness and other details of its fossil bones, teeth, claws and other parts.

The tail of *T rex* was almost half its total length. It had a wide, muscular base and was thick and strong almost to the tip, quite unlike the long, thin, whip-like tails of other dinosaurs such as *Diplodocus*.

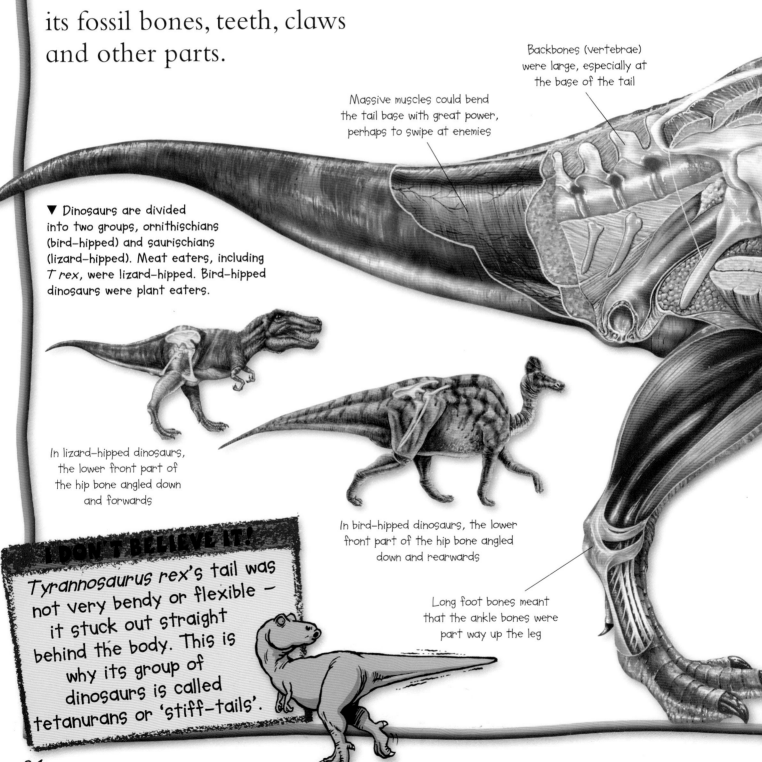

Backbones (vertebrae) were large, especially at the base of the tail

Massive muscles could bend the tail base with great power, perhaps to swipe at enemies

▼ Dinosaurs are divided into two groups, ornithischians (bird-hipped) and saurischians (lizard-hipped). Meat eaters, including *T rex*, were lizard-hipped. Bird-hipped dinosaurs were plant eaters.

In lizard-hipped dinosaurs, the lower front part of the hip bone angled down and forwards

In bird-hipped dinosaurs, the lower front part of the hip bone angled down and rearwards

Long foot bones meant that the ankle bones were part way up the leg

I DON'T BELIEVE IT!

Tyrannosaurus rex's tail was not very bendy or flexible – it stuck out straight behind the body. This is why its group of dinosaurs is called tetanurans or 'stiff-tails'.

The fossil bones of *T rex* show that it was a large, heavily built, powerful dinosaur. It had a huge skull, so its head and mouth were massive. There were holes in the skull for the eyes, ears and nasal openings or nostrils. There were also smaller holes in the bones for blood vessels and nerves.

▼ A cutaway *T rex* shows the thick, strong bones of its skeleton, which have been found preserved in many different fossil remains.

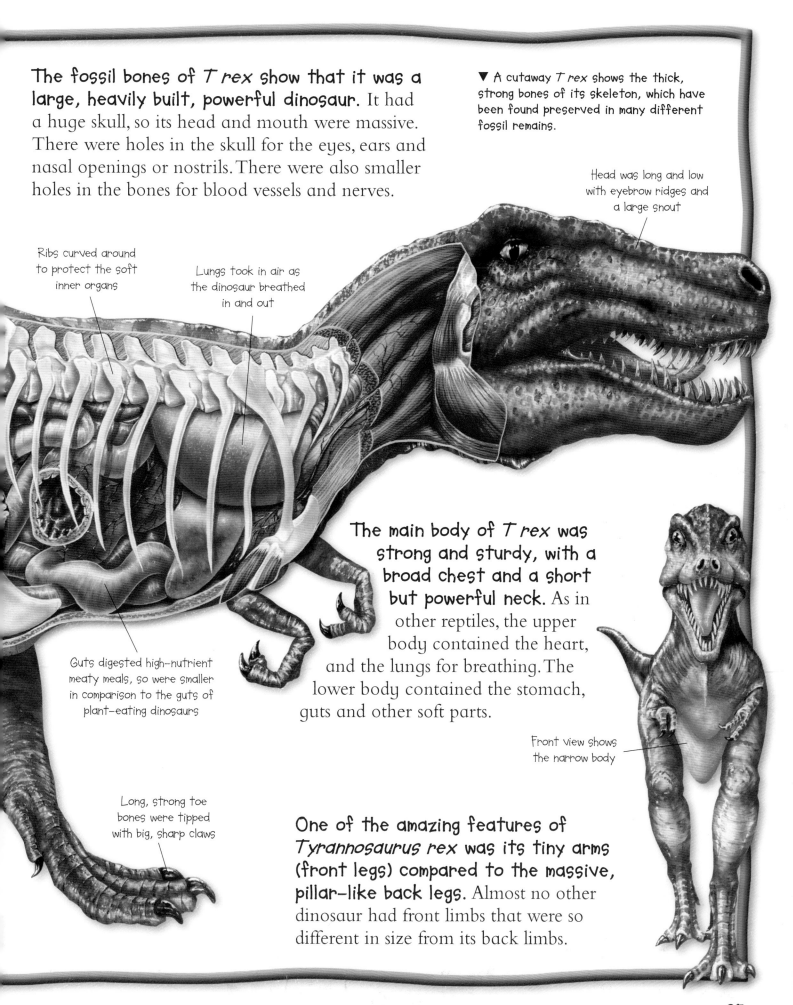

Head was long and low with eyebrow ridges and a large snout

Ribs curved around to protect the soft inner organs

Lungs took in air as the dinosaur breathed in and out

The main body of *T rex* was strong and sturdy, with a broad chest and a short but powerful neck. As in other reptiles, the upper body contained the heart, and the lungs for breathing. The lower body contained the stomach, guts and other soft parts.

Guts digested high–nutrient meaty meals, so were smaller in comparison to the guts of plant–eating dinosaurs

Front view shows the narrow body

Long, strong toe bones were tipped with big, sharp claws

One of the amazing features of *Tyrannosaurus rex* was its tiny arms (front legs) compared to the massive, pillar–like back legs. Almost no other dinosaur had front limbs that were so different in size from its back limbs.

Was T rex clever?

▼ Many dinosaurs had eyes on the sides of the head, giving good all-round vision but not a detailed front view. *T rex* had forward-facing eyes.

View from forward-facing eyes

View from sideways-facing eyes

▶ *T rex* probably used its long tongue to lick and taste meat before it started to eat.

The skull of *T rex* is well known from several good fossils. They show that the large eyes were set at an angle so they looked forwards rather than to the sides. This allowed *T rex* to see an object in front with both eyes and judge its distance well.

As far as we know dinosaurs, like other reptiles, lacked ear flaps. Instead, they had eardrums of thin skin on the sides of their heads so they could hear.

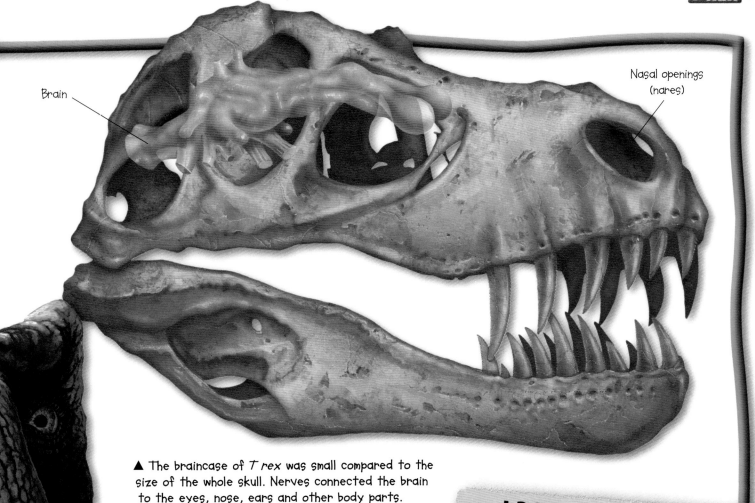

Brain

Nasal openings (nares)

▲ The braincase of *T rex* was small compared to the size of the whole skull. Nerves connected the brain to the eyes, nose, ears and other body parts.

T rex's big nasal openings were at the top of its snout. They opened into a very large chamber inside the skull, which detected smells floating in the air. *T rex*'s sense of smell, like its eyesight, was very good.

I DON'T BELIEVE IT!

The eyeballs of *Tyrannosaurus rex* were up to 8 centimetres across – but those of today's giant squid are almost 30 centimetres!

Some fossils even show the size and shape of *T rex*'s brain! The brain was in a casing called the cranium in the upper rear of the skull. This can be seen in well-preserved skulls. The space inside shows the brain's shape.

Tyrannosaurus rex had the biggest brain of almost any dinosaur. The parts dealing with the sense of smell, called the olfactory lobes, were especially large. So *T rex* had keen senses of sight, hearing and especially smell. And it wasn't stupid.

What big teeth!

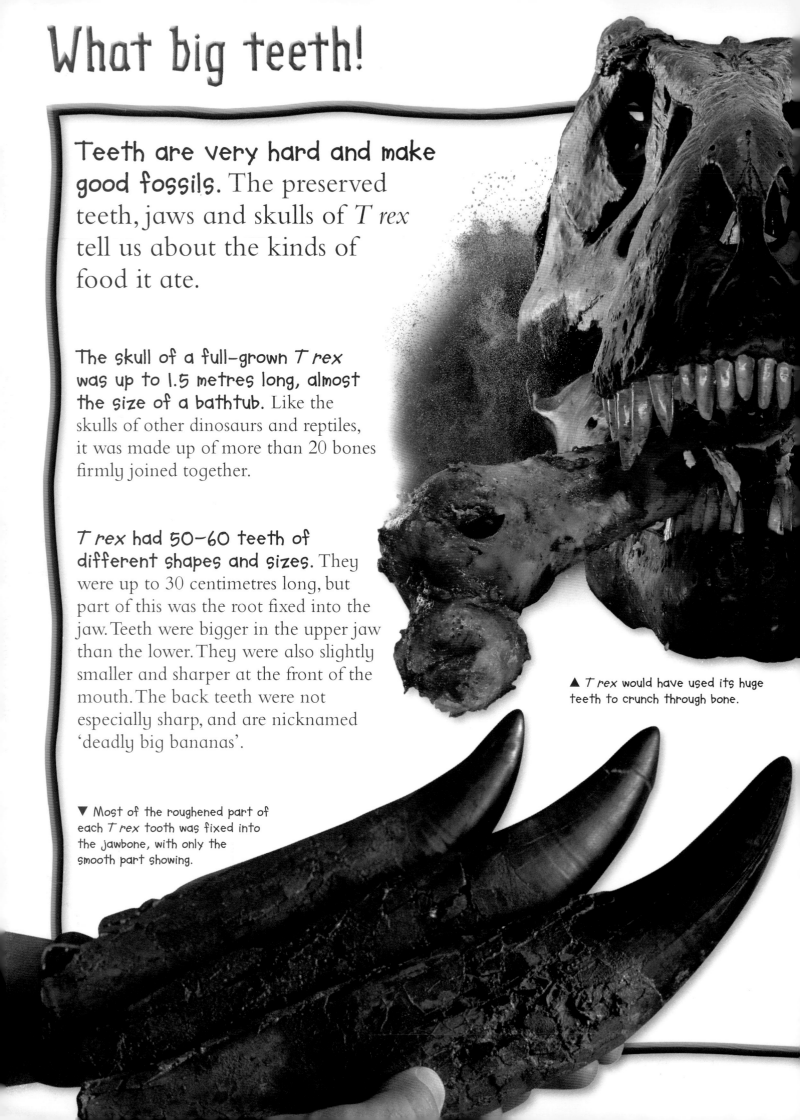

Teeth are very hard and make good fossils. The preserved teeth, jaws and skulls of *T rex* tell us about the kinds of food it ate.

The skull of a full-grown *T rex* was up to 1.5 metres long, almost the size of a bathtub. Like the skulls of other dinosaurs and reptiles, it was made up of more than 20 bones firmly joined together.

***T rex* had 50–60 teeth of different shapes and sizes.** They were up to 30 centimetres long, but part of this was the root fixed into the jaw. Teeth were bigger in the upper jaw than the lower. They were also slightly smaller and sharper at the front of the mouth. The back teeth were not especially sharp, and are nicknamed 'deadly big bananas'.

▶ *T rex* would have used its huge teeth to crunch through bone.

▼ Most of the roughened part of each *T rex* tooth was fixed into the jawbone, with only the smooth part showing.

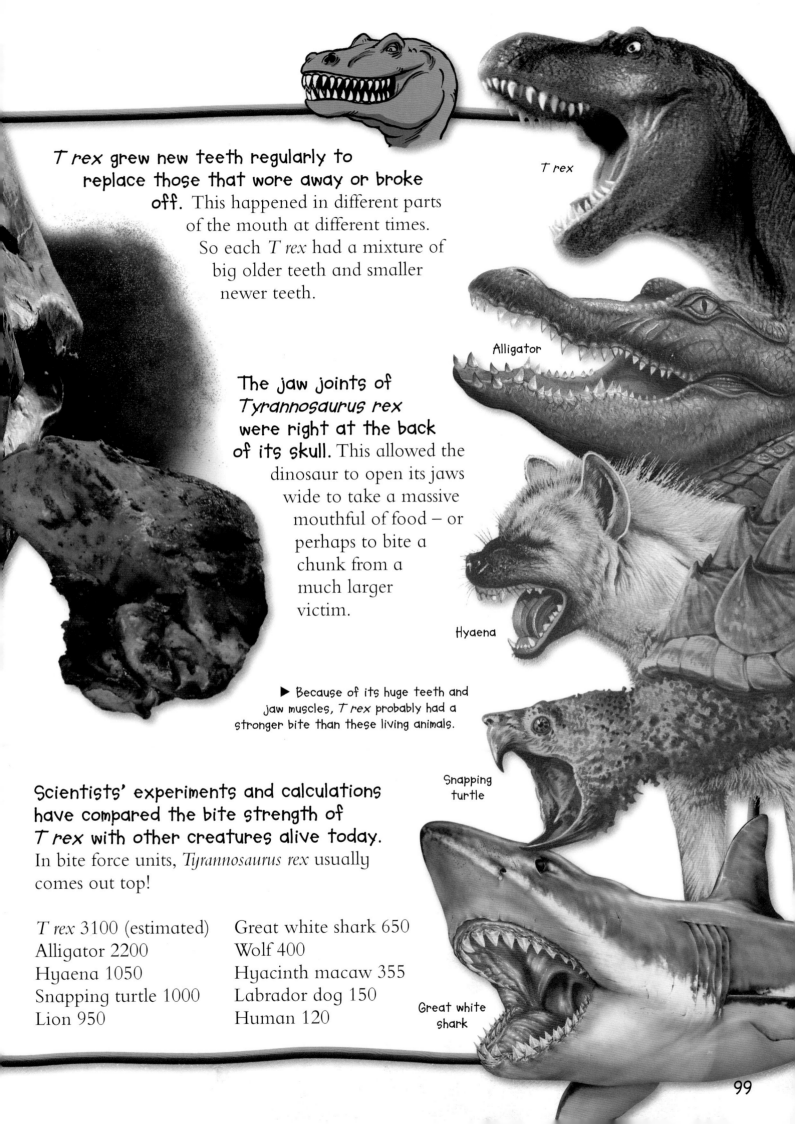

T rex grew new teeth regularly to replace those that wore away or broke off. This happened in different parts of the mouth at different times. So each *T rex* had a mixture of big older teeth and smaller newer teeth.

T rex

Alligator

The jaw joints of *Tyrannosaurus rex* were right at the back of its skull. This allowed the dinosaur to open its jaws wide to take a massive mouthful of food – or perhaps to bite a chunk from a much larger victim.

Hyaena

▶ Because of its huge teeth and jaw muscles, *T rex* probably had a stronger bite than these living animals.

Snapping turtle

Scientists' experiments and calculations have compared the bite strength of *T rex* with other creatures alive today. In bite force units, *Tyrannosaurus rex* usually comes out top!

T rex 3100 (estimated)
Alligator 2200
Hyaena 1050
Snapping turtle 1000
Lion 950

Great white shark 650
Wolf 400
Hyacinth macaw 355
Labrador dog 150
Human 120

Great white shark

Tiny arms, big legs

Tyrannosaurus rex's strangest features were its tiny arms. In fact, they were about the same size as the arms of an adult human, even though *T rex* was more than 50 times bigger than a person. Yet the arms were not weak. They had powerful muscles and two strong clawed fingers.

▶ *T rex*'s arms were so small, they could not even be used for passing food to the mouth.

What did Tyrannosaurus rex use its mini-arms for? There have been many suggestions such as holding onto a victim while biting, pushing itself off the ground if it fell over, and holding onto a partner at breeding time. Perhaps we will never know the true reason.

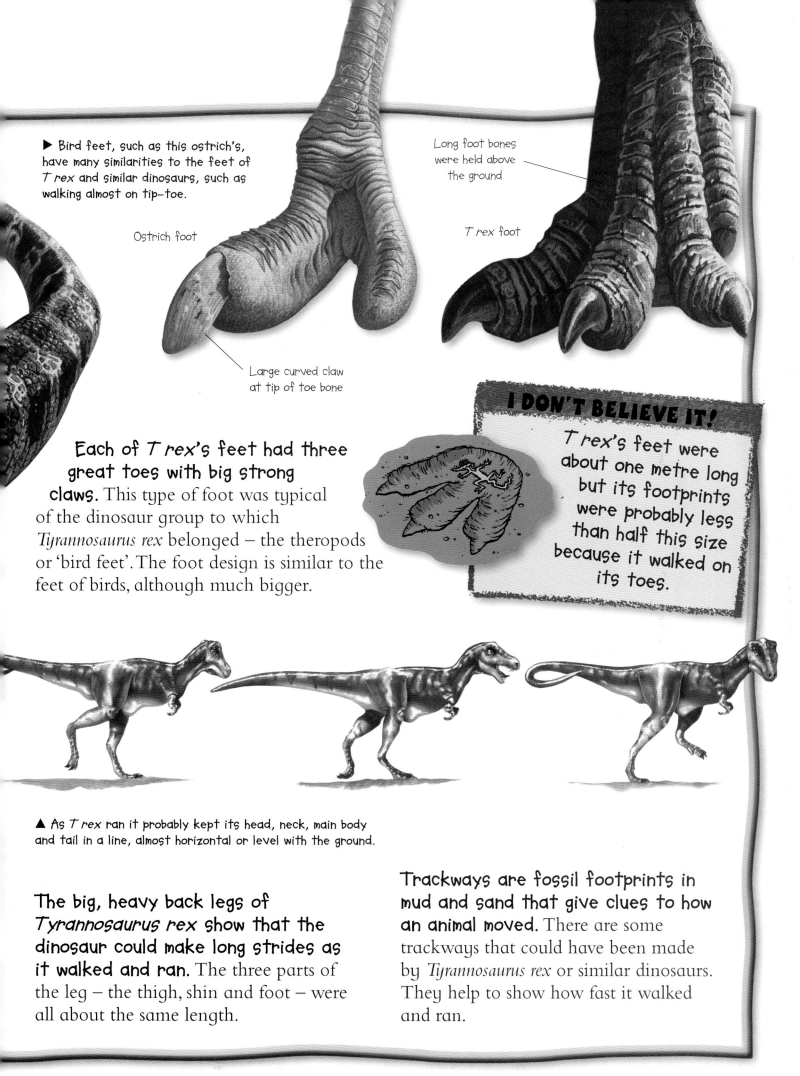

▶ Bird feet, such as this ostrich's, have many similarities to the feet of *T rex* and similar dinosaurs, such as walking almost on tip-toe.

Ostrich foot

Long foot bones were held above the ground

T rex foot

Large curved claw at tip of toe bone

Each of *T rex*'s feet had three great toes with big strong claws. This type of foot was typical of the dinosaur group to which *Tyrannosaurus rex* belonged – the theropods or 'bird feet'. The foot design is similar to the feet of birds, although much bigger.

▲ As *T rex* ran it probably kept its head, neck, main body and tail in a line, almost horizontal or level with the ground.

The big, heavy back legs of *Tyrannosaurus rex* show that the dinosaur could make long strides as it walked and ran. The three parts of the leg – the thigh, shin and foot – were all about the same length.

Trackways are fossil footprints in mud and sand that give clues to how an animal moved. There are some trackways that could have been made by *Tyrannosaurus rex* or similar dinosaurs. They help to show how fast it walked and ran.

What did T rex eat?

Tyrannosaurus rex was a huge hunter, so it probably ate big prey. Other large dinosaurs of its time and place were plant eaters. They included three-horned *Triceratops* and its cousins, and various 'duckbilled' dinosaurs (hadrosaurs) such as *Parasaurolophus* and *Edmontosaurus*.

▼ The giant pterosaur (flying reptile) *Quetzalcoatlus* lived at about the same time as *T rex*. It may have pecked at the remains of a *T rex* kill after the dinosaur had finished feasting.

T rex could have used its huge mouth, strong teeth and powerful jaw muscles to attack these big plant eaters. It may have lunged at a victim with one massive bite to cause a slashing wound. Then it would retreat a short distance and wait for the prey to weaken from blood loss before moving in to feed.

◄ An adult *Triceratops* would be a fierce foe for *T rex* to tackle. However young, sick and old *Triceratops* might have been easier to kill.

One fossil of *Triceratops* has scratch-like gouge marks on its large, bony neck frill. These could have been made by *Tyrannosaurus rex* teeth. The marks are about the correct distance apart, matching the spacing of *T rex* teeth.

▶ The hadrosaur *Parasaurolophus* might have made loud trumpeting noises through its hollow tube-like head crest, to warn others in its herd that *T rex* was near.

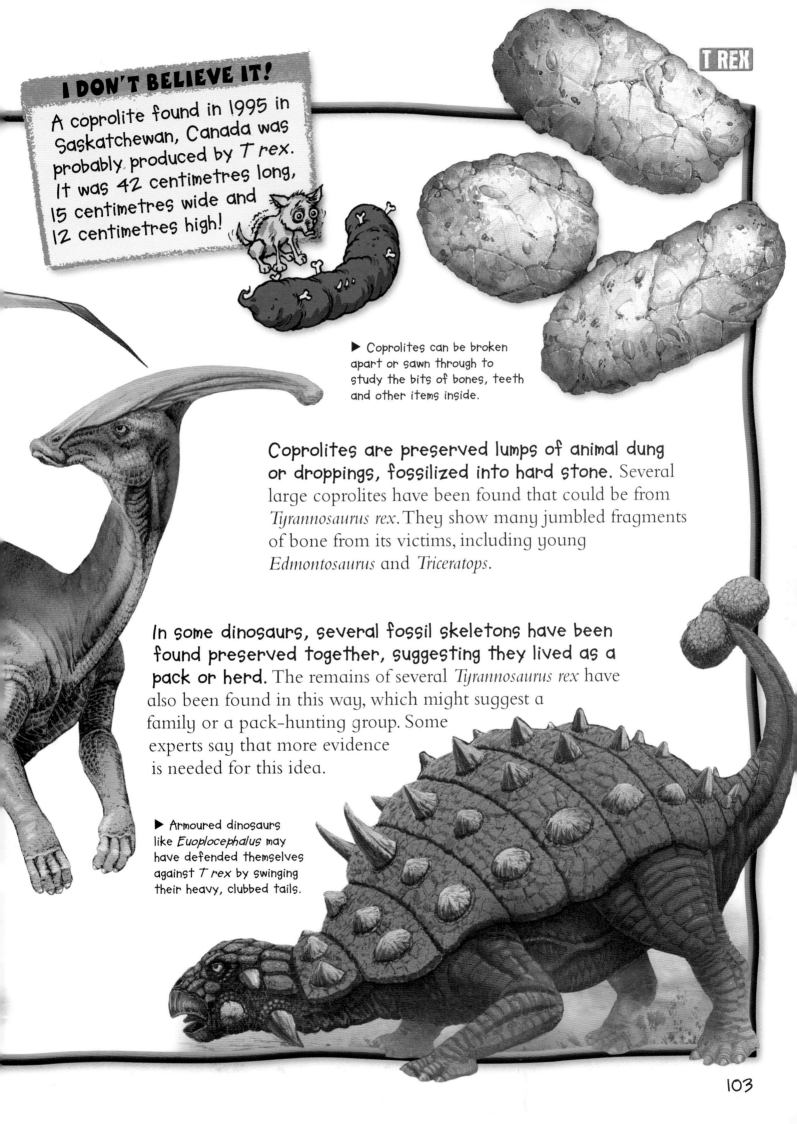

▶ Coprolites can be broken apart or sawn through to study the bits of bones, teeth and other items inside.

Coprolites are preserved lumps of animal dung or droppings, fossilized into hard stone. Several large coprolites have been found that could be from *Tyrannosaurus rex*. They show many jumbled fragments of bone from its victims, including young *Edmontosaurus* and *Triceratops*.

In some dinosaurs, several fossil skeletons have been found preserved together, suggesting they lived as a pack or herd. The remains of several *Tyrannosaurus rex* have also been found in this way, which might suggest a family or a pack-hunting group. Some experts say that more evidence is needed for this idea.

▶ Armoured dinosaurs like *Euoplocephalus* may have defended themselves against T rex by swinging their heavy, clubbed tails.

Hunter or scavenger?

Was *T rex* an active hunter that chased after its victims? Was it an ambush predator that hid in wait to rush out at prey? Was it a scavenger that ate any dead or dying dinosaurs it found? Or did it chase other dinosaurs from their kills and steal the meal for itself?

To be an active pursuit hunter, *T rex* must have been able to run fast. Scientists have tried to work out its running speed using models and computers, and by comparisons with other animals.

Who does what?

Research these animals living today and find out if they are mainly fast hunters, sneaky ambushers or scavengers.
Tiger Cheetah Hyaena
Crocodile Vulture
African wild dog

▶ *Tyrannosaurus rex* may have run down smaller dinosaurs such as these *Prenocephale*, perhaps rushing out from its hiding place in a clump of trees.

▲ When scavenging, *T rex* might sniff out a dinosaur that had died from illness or injury.

▲ When hunting, *T rex* would be at risk from injury, such as from the horns of *Triceratops*.

Some estimates for the running speed of *T rex* are as fast as 50 kilometres an hour, others are as slow as 15 kilometres an hour. Most give a speed of between 20 and 30 kilometres an hour. This is slightly slower than a human sprinter, but probably faster than typical *T rex* prey such as *Triceratops*.

Several *T rex* fossils show injuries to body parts such as shins, ribs, neck and jaws. These could have been made by victims fighting back, suggesting that *T rex* hunted live prey.

▶ *T rex* would tear and rip flesh from large prey, gulp in lumps and swallow them whole.

Evidence that *T rex* was a scavenger includes its very well developed sense of smell for sniffing out dead, rotting bodies. Also, its powerful teeth could not chew food repeatedly like we do, but they could crush bones at first bite to get at the nutritious jelly-like marrow inside. Maybe a hungry *Tyrannosaurus rex* simply ate anything it could catch or find, so it was a hunter, ambusher and scavenger all in one.

Growing up

Did *T rex* live in groups? Most of its fossils are of lone individuals. Some were found near other specimens of *T rex*. These could have been preserved near each other by chance, or they could have been a group that all died together.

Embryo

Yolk

▲ A baby dinosaur developed as an embryo in its egg, fed by nutrients from the yolk.

▶ The baby probably hatched out by biting through the tough shell, which was flexible like leather.

Living reptiles lay eggs that hatch into young, and dinosaurs such as *T rex* probably did the same. Many fossil dinosaur eggs have been discovered, but none are known for certain to be from *T rex*. Some dinosaurs laid eggs in nests and looked after their young, but again there are no fossils like this for *T rex*.

It seems that *T rex* grew slowly for about 12–14 years. Then suddenly it grew very fast, putting on about 2 kilograms every day as a teenager. By 20 years it was full-grown.

▶ Young *T rex* may have killed small prey such as birds, lizards and newly hatched dinosaurs.

Fossils of individual *T rex* are of different sizes and ages, showing how this dinosaur grew up. Some of the fossil bones are so well preserved that they have 'growth rings' almost like a tree trunk, showing growth speed.

Can we tell apart female and male *Tyrannosaurus rex* from their fossils? Some scientists thought that females were bigger, with stronger, thicker bones than the males. However the latest evidence makes this less clear.

▶ In many reptiles today, the adults keep growing with age. However their growth rate gradually reduces, so they get bigger more slowly. It is not certain if dinosaurs such as *T rex* grew like this.

The biggest *T rex* found, 'Sue', was about 28 years old when it died. No one knows for certain if *Tyrannosaurus rex* could live longer. As with many of these questions, more fossil finds will help to fill in the details.

Where in the world?

T rex was one kind, or species, of dinosaur in a group of species known as the genus *Tyrannosaurus*. Were there any other members of this genus?

After *T rex* fossils were discovered and named over 100 years ago, fossil-hunters began to find the remains of many similar huge predators. Some were given their own names in the genus *Tyrannosaurus*, but most have now been renamed *Tyrannosaurus rex*.

Tarbosaurus, 'terrifying lizard', was very similar to *T rex*, almost as big, and it lived at the same time. However its fossils come from Asia – Mongolia and China – rather than North America. Some experts consider it to be another species of *Tyrannosaurus*, called *Tyrannosaurus bataar*. Others think that it's so similar to *T rex* that it should be called *Tyrannosaurus rex*.

Fossils of smaller dinosaurs similar to *T rex* have been found in Europe. They include 6-metre-long *Eotyrannus*, from more than 100 million years ago, from the Isle of Wight, southern England. Fossils of *Aviatyrannis* from Portugal are even older, from the Jurassic Period.

◀ *Tarbosaurus* had big teeth, tiny arms and many other features similar to *T rex*. It was named by Russian fossil expert Evgeny Maleev in 1955, exactly 50 years after *T rex* was named.

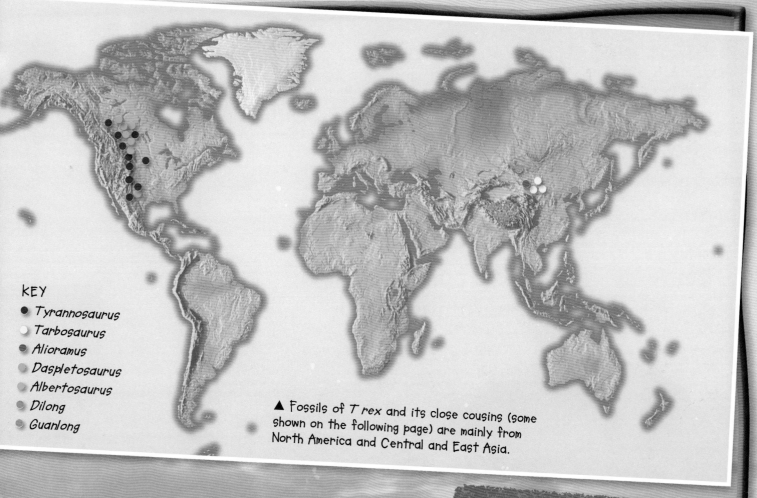

KEY
- Tyrannosaurus
- Tarbosaurus
- Alioramus
- Daspletosaurus
- Albertosaurus
- Dilong
- Guanlong

▲ Fossils of T rex and its close cousins (some shown on the following page) are mainly from North America and Central and East Asia.

In 1979, Chinese expert Dong Zhiming named the remains of a big Asian meat-eating dinosaur as *Tyrannosaurus luanchuanensis*, in the same genus as *Tyrannosaurus rex*. After much discussion another name was suggested – *Jenghizkhan*. However some scientists say that like *Tarbosaurus*, *Jenghizkhan* is so similar to *T rex* that it should be called *Tyrannosaurus*.

I DON'T BELIEVE IT!

A fossil skull found in 1942 was named *Nanotyrannus*, 'tiny tyrant'. It may be a separate kind of small tyrannosaur – or simply a young T rex. Experts are undecided.

Tyrannosaur group

What kind of dinosaur was *Tyrannosaurus rex*? It belonged to the group called tyrannosaurs, known scientifically as the family *Tyrannosauridae*. These dinosaurs had bones, joints and other features that were different from other predatory dinosaurs. They were part of an even bigger group, the tyrannosauroids.

Tyrannosaurus rex

Nanotyrannus (could be same as Tyrannosaurus)

Tarbosaurus (could be same as Tyrannosaurus)

Tyrannosaurine subfamily

One of the first tyrannosauroids was *Guanlong*, 'crown dragon'. Its fossils were discovered in China in 2006 and are about 160 million years old – nearly 100 million years before *Tyrannosaurus rex*. It was 3 metres long and had a strange horn-like plate of bone on its nose.

▲ *Guanlong* may have shown off the crest of thin bone on its head to possible partners at breeding time.

▼ The 'feathers' of *Dilong* were similar to fur and may have kept its body warm.

Another early cousin of *T rex* was *Dilong*, 'emperor dragon', also from China. Its fossils date to 130 million years ago. *Dilong* was about 2 metres long when fully grown. It had traces of hair-like feathers on the head and tail. As shown later, some experts suggest *Tyrannosaurus rex* itself may have had some kind of feathers.

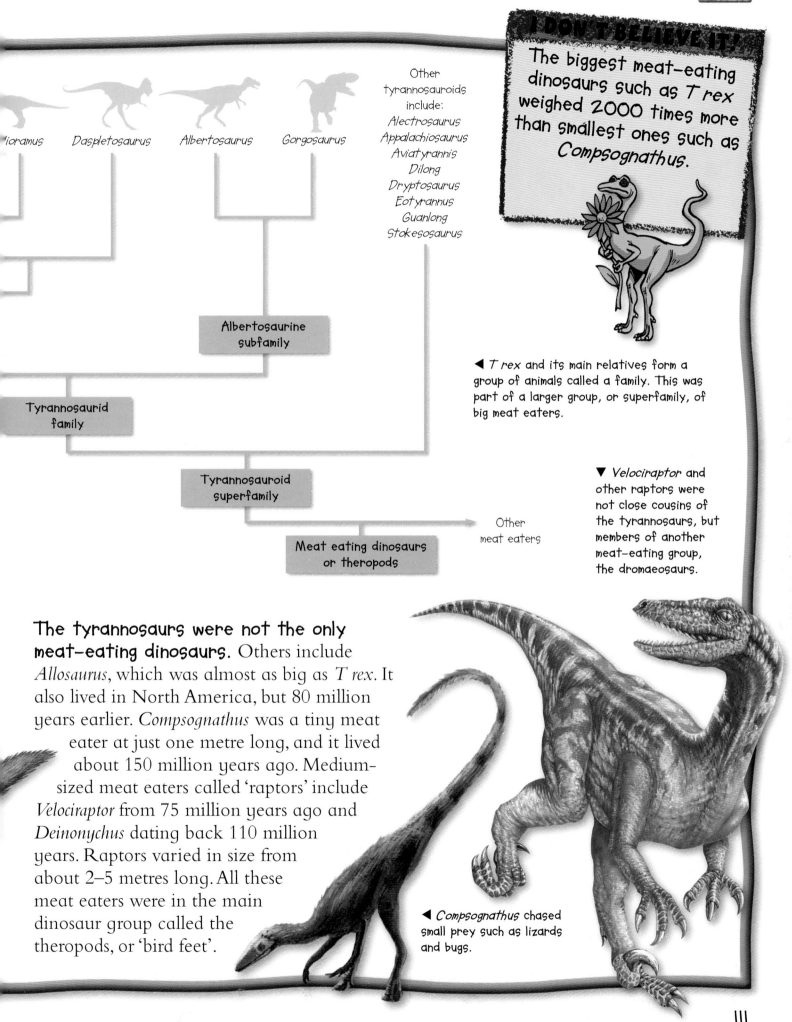

ioramus   Daspletosaurus   Albertosaurus   Gorgosaurus

Other
tyrannosauroids
include:
Alectrosaurus
Appalachiosaurus
Aviatyrannis
Dilong
Dryptosaurus
Eotyrannus
Guanlong
Stokesosaurus

Albertosaurine
subfamily

Tyrannosaurid
family

Tyrannosauroid
superfamily

Other
meat eaters

Meat eating dinosaurs
or theropods

I DON'T BELIEVE IT!

The biggest meat-eating dinosaurs such as T rex weighed 2000 times more than smallest ones such as Compsognathus.

◀ T rex and its main relatives form a group of animals called a family. This was part of a larger group, or superfamily, of big meat eaters.

▼ Velociraptor and other raptors were not close cousins of the tyrannosaurs, but members of another meat-eating group, the dromaeosaurs.

The tyrannosaurs were not the only meat-eating dinosaurs. Others include *Allosaurus*, which was almost as big as *T rex*. It also lived in North America, but 80 million years earlier. *Compsognathus* was a tiny meat eater at just one metre long, and it lived about 150 million years ago. Medium-sized meat eaters called 'raptors' include *Velociraptor* from 75 million years ago and *Deinonychus* dating back 110 million years. Raptors varied in size from about 2–5 metres long. All these meat eaters were in the main dinosaur group called the theropods, or 'bird feet'.

◀ *Compsognathus* chased small prey such as lizards and bugs.

Close cousins

In the tyrannosaur group with *T rex* were several of its closest relatives. They were big, fierce dinosaurs, but most lived before *T rex* and were not quite as large.

▲ There are many fossil remains of *Gorgosaurus*, making it one of the best known of all the tyrannosaurs. It had a small horn-like crest above each eye.

Fossils of *Gorgosaurus*, 'fierce lizard', come mainly from Alberta, Canada and are 75–70 million years old. *Gorgosaurus* was very similar to *Albertosaurus*, although slightly smaller at 8–9 metres long. Like all tyrannosaurs, it had hollow bones and openings in its skull that helped to reduce its weight. Some experts think that *Gorgosaurus* was really a kind of *Albertosaurus* and that its name should be changed.

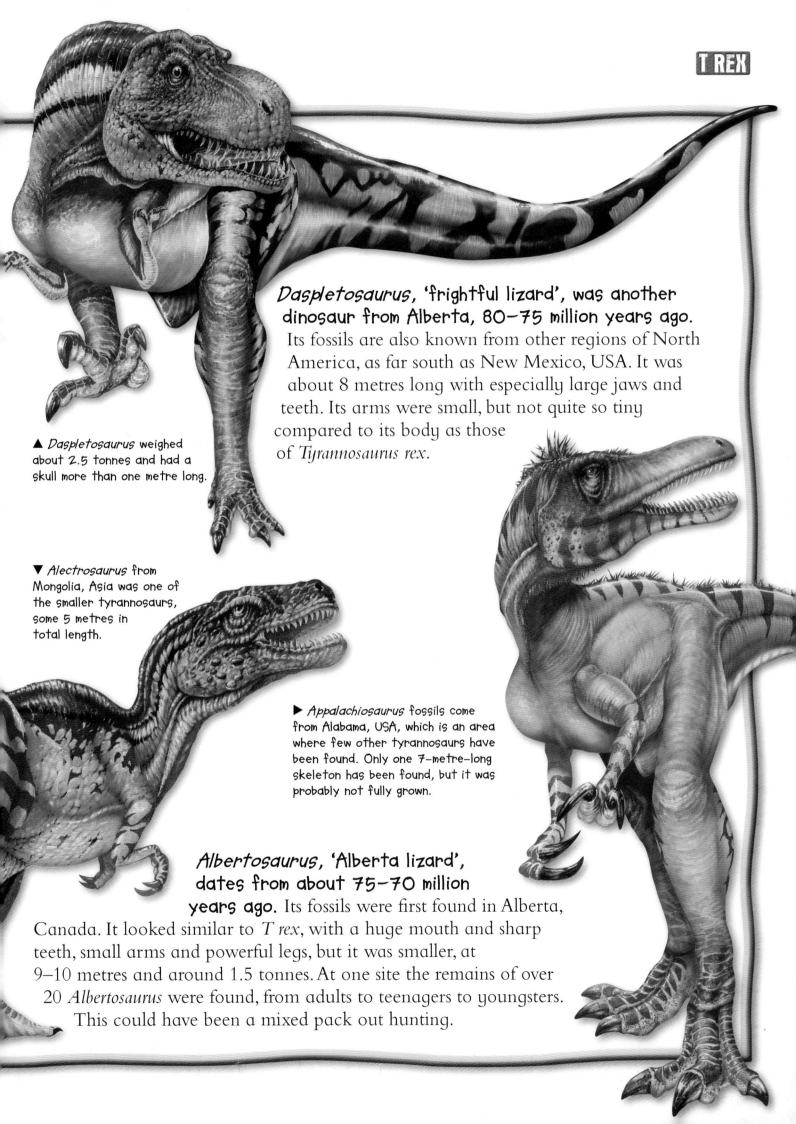

Daspletosaurus, 'frightful lizard', was another dinosaur from Alberta, 80–75 million years ago. Its fossils are also known from other regions of North America, as far south as New Mexico, USA. It was about 8 metres long with especially large jaws and teeth. Its arms were small, but not quite so tiny compared to its body as those of *Tyrannosaurus rex*.

▲ *Daspletosaurus* weighed about 2.5 tonnes and had a skull more than one metre long.

▼ *Alectrosaurus* from Mongolia, Asia was one of the smaller tyrannosaurs, some 5 metres in total length.

▶ *Appalachiosaurus* fossils come from Alabama, USA, which is an area where few other tyrannosaurs have been found. Only one 7-metre-long skeleton has been found, but it was probably not fully grown.

Albertosaurus, 'Alberta lizard', dates from about 75–70 million years ago. Its fossils were first found in Alberta, Canada. It looked similar to *T rex*, with a huge mouth and sharp teeth, small arms and powerful legs, but it was smaller, at 9–10 metres and around 1.5 tonnes. At one site the remains of over 20 *Albertosaurus* were found, from adults to teenagers to youngsters. This could have been a mixed pack out hunting.

Discovering T rex

The first fossils of *T rex* were found in the 1870s by Arthur Lakes and John Bell Hatcher, in Wyoming, USA. However these were not recognized as *T rex* until years later. In 1892, fossil expert Edward Drinker Cope found remains of a big meat eater and named them *Manospondylus*. Over 100 years later these remains were restudied and renamed as *T rex*.

▲ Edward Drinker Cope (1840–97) named many other kinds of dinosaurs in addition to *T rex*, including *Camarasaurus*, *Amphicoelias*, *Coelophysis*, *Hadrosaurus* and *Monoclonius*.

▶ The fossil bones of big dinosaurs such as *T rex* are solid stone and very heavy. Many years ago, horses dragged them from rocky, remote areas to the nearest road or railway.

In 1900, again in Wyoming, leading fossil collector Barnum Brown found the first partial skeleton of *Tyrannosaurus rex*, rather than scattered single bones and teeth. At first the fossils were named as *Dynamosaurus* by Henry Fairfield Osborn of the American Museum of Natural History in New York.

T rex fossils have always been greatly prized by museums, exhibitions and private collectors. In 1941, the fossils that Brown found in 1902 were sold to the Carnegie Museum of Natural History in Pittsburgh, Pennsylvania, for a huge sum of money. Searching for, selling and buying *T rex* fossils continues today.

▼ Barnum Brown was the most famous fossil-hunter of his time. He sometimes wore a thick fur coat — even when digging for fossils in the scorching sun.

Barnum Brown discovered parts of another *Tyrannosaurus rex* fossil skeleton at Hell Creek, Montana, in 1902. In 1905, Osborn wrote a scientific description of these remains and called them *Tyrannosaurus rex*. This was the first time the official name was used. In a way, it was when *T rex* was 'born'.

In 1906, Brown found an even better part-skeleton of *Tyrannosaurus rex* in Montana. The same year, Osborn realized that the *Dynamosaurus* fossils were extremely similar to *Tyrannosaurus rex*, so he renamed those too as *Tyrannosaurus rex*. The public began to hear about this huge, fierce, meat-eating monster from long ago, and soon its fame was growing fast.

BARNUM BROWN — DINOSAUR DETECTIVE

Barnum Brown (1873-1963) collected not only dinosaur fossils, but fossils of all kinds, and other scientific treasures such as crystals. He and his teams worked for the American Museum of Natural History in New York. They travelled to remote places, and if there were rivers but no roads, they used a large raft as a floating base camp. They worked fast too, often blasting apart rocks with dynamite. Brown also made a living by informing oil companies about the best places to drill for oil.

Working with fossils

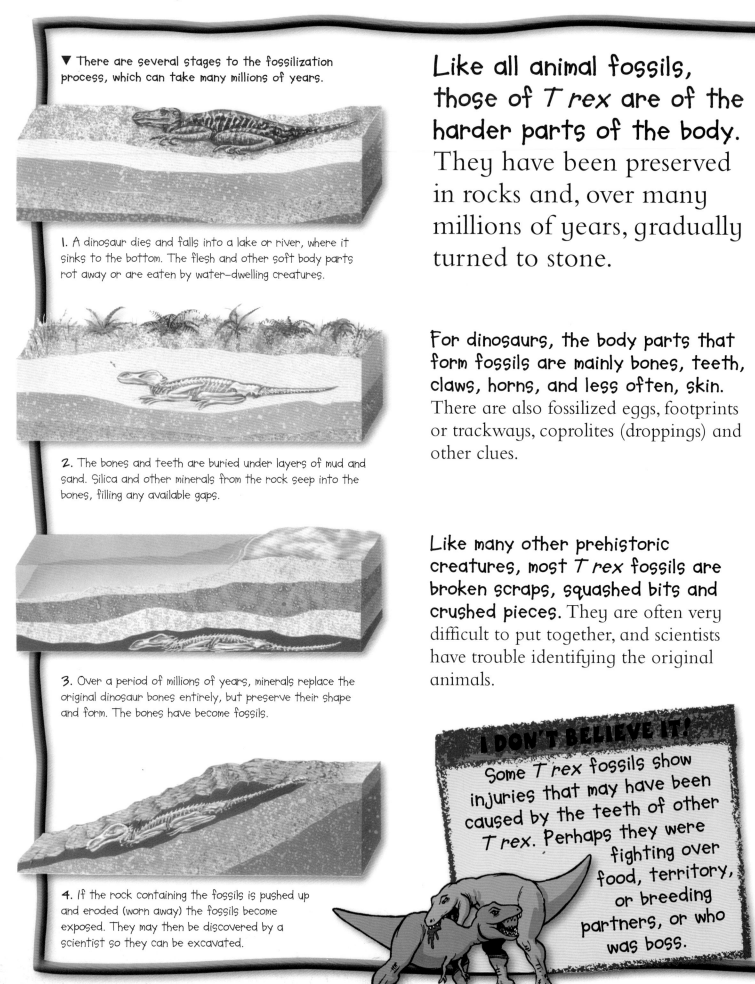

▼ There are several stages to the fossilization process, which can take many millions of years.

1. A dinosaur dies and falls into a lake or river, where it sinks to the bottom. The flesh and other soft body parts rot away or are eaten by water-dwelling creatures.

2. The bones and teeth are buried under layers of mud and sand. Silica and other minerals from the rock seep into the bones, filling any available gaps.

3. Over a period of millions of years, minerals replace the original dinosaur bones entirely, but preserve their shape and form. The bones have become fossils.

4. If the rock containing the fossils is pushed up and eroded (worn away) the fossils become exposed. They may then be discovered by a scientist so they can be excavated.

Like all animal fossils, those of *T rex* are of the harder parts of the body. They have been preserved in rocks and, over many millions of years, gradually turned to stone.

For dinosaurs, the body parts that form fossils are mainly bones, teeth, claws, horns, and less often, skin. There are also fossilized eggs, footprints or trackways, coprolites (droppings) and other clues.

Like many other prehistoric creatures, most *T rex* fossils are broken scraps, squashed bits and crushed pieces. They are often very difficult to put together, and scientists have trouble identifying the original animals.

I DON'T BELIEVE IT!

Some *T rex* fossils show injuries that may have been caused by the teeth of other *T rex*. Perhaps they were fighting over food, territory, or breeding partners, or who was boss.

▶ *Archaeopteryx*, the earliest known bird, lived about 80 million years before *T rex*. Its bones show many similarities to small meat-eating dinosaurs.

Reptiles today are cold-blooded, but were *T rex* and some other dinosaurs warm-blooded, like mammals and birds? Fossils show that *T rex*'s bone structure and growth rate were similar to mammals and birds. There is also evidence that the chemical make-up of its preserved bones resembles birds. But there is no complete proof one way or the other.

▶ A palaeontologist working at a *T rex* dig site. A variety of tools and special equipment is needed to help remove the fossils from the ground.

In 2008, 68-million-year-old fossils of *T rex* (named 'B rex' by palaeontologists) were unearthed in Montana, USA. Examining these very well-preserved bones with a microscope showed they were similar to those of living female birds. So 'B rex' may well have been a female *T rex* producing eggs inside her body when she died aged 15–20 years.

Rebuilding T rex

Fossil experts use preserved bones and other parts of *T rex* to show what it looked like when alive. The bones are also compared to those of similar animals alive today, known as comparative anatomy. For *T rex*, similar living animals include crocodiles, lizards – and birds.

As with other extinct creatures, there are no remains of *T rex*'s soft body parts such as the stomach, guts, heart and lungs. These were eaten by scavengers soon after death or were rotted away. However experts can use comparative anatomy with living creatures to imagine what *T rex*'s soft body parts looked like.

▼ Fossil dinosaur skin has a scaly surface, similar to many of today's reptiles.

Some fossil bones have patches, grooves and ridges called 'muscle scars'. They show where the animal's muscles were joined to the bones in life. This helps experts to work out how the muscles pulled the bones and how *T rex* moved when it was alive.

Skin and scales of dinosaurs sometimes form fossils. However they are the colour of the rocks that make the fossils, not the colour of the original skin and scales. So we have no way of knowing *T rex*'s true colour in life.

◄ Close cousins of *T rex* have been preserved with simple hair-like feathers on their skin. It may be possible that *T rex* also had feathers.

▲ This reconstruction of *T rex* shows the modern idea of its body position, with tail held straight out behind. When the skull is moved from the trolley to the front end of the neck bones, it will be positioned low, not high as previously thought.

▶ For many years, *T rex* was thought to hold its head up high and drag its tail along the ground.

The first reconstructions of *T rex* showed it standing almost upright like a kangaroo. However from its bone and joint shapes, most experts now think that it held its head and body level with the ground, balanced over its big back legs by its long, heavy tail.

119

The story of Sue

The biggest *Tyrannosaurus rex* found so far is 'Sue'. Its official code number is FMNH PR2081, from the Field Museum of Natural History in Chicago, USA.

'Sue' is named after its discoverer, Sue Hendrickson. She was working at a fossil dig in 1990 near the town of Faith, in South Dakota, USA, when she uncovered parts of a massive *T rex*. An entire team of people helped to dig up and clean the remains.

'Sue' is amazingly complete for a fossil animal, with about four-fifths of its teeth, bones and other parts preserved. The dinosaur was probably covered with mud soon after it died, which prevented scavenging animals from cracking open or carrying away its bones.

'Sue' dates from between 67 and 65.5 million years ago. It measures 12.8 metres from nose to tail-tip and 4 metres tall at the hips. The weight of 'Sue' when alive was probably between 5.5 and 6.5 tonnes.

◀ Sue Hendrickson with the fossil foot of 'Sue'. As well as finding 'Sue' the *T rex*, Sue Hendrickson is an expert diver and has explored shipwrecks and sunken cities.

◀ In May 2000, 'Sue' went on display at the Field Museum of Chicago and has been the star attraction ever since.

After 'Sue' was discovered, there was a dispute about who owned the fossils. Various people claimed them, including the landowner, the dig team, the organizers of the excavation and the local authorities. After a legal battle, 'Sue' was sold at auction in 1997 in New York. The Field Museum of Chicago paid $8.39 million.

Stan, Jane and the rest

Apart from 'Sue', there are more than 30 other sets of *T rex* fossils. Some are just a few bones and teeth, while others are well preserved, fairly complete skeletons.

'Wankel rex', specimen MOR 555, was found by Kathy Wankel in 1988. It was excavated by a team from the Museum of the Rockies and is now on show at that museum in Bozeman, Montana.

'Tinker', also called 'Kid Rex', was a young *Tyrannosaurus rex*. About two-thirds adult size, it was found in 1998 in South Dakota and named after the leader of the fossil-hunting team, Ron 'Tinker' Frithiof.

'Stan' is named after its discoverer Stan Sacrisen. Code numbered BHI 3033, it was dug up near Buffalo, South Dakota, USA in 1992 by a team from the Black Hills Institute. 'Stan' was about 12.2 metres long and 3 tonnes in weight, with 199 bones and 58 teeth. Some bones show signs of injuries that had healed, including broken ribs, a damaged neck and a tooth wound in the skull.

▶ 'Stan' is now at the Black Hills Museum in Hill City, South Dakota.

'Jane' is specimen BMRP 2002.4.1 at the Burpee Museum of Natural History, Rockford, Illinois, USA. Found in Montana, it's smaller than a full grown *Tyrannosaurus rex*, at 6.5 metres long and 650–700 kilograms. Some experts believe it is a part-grown youngster, probably 10–12 years old when it died. Others say it is a similar but smaller kind of dinosaur named *Nanotyrannus*.

▶ The fossils of 'Jane' from Montana's Hell Creek took more than four years to dig out, clean up and put together for display.

A new name for T rex

You will need:
pictures of *T rex* in different poses
pen   paper

Copy some pictures of *T rex* onto your paper. Imagine you and your friends have discovered their fossils and given them nicknames. Write these next to your drawings. Perhaps *T rex* should be named after you?

Bigger than the 'King'

Until the 1990s, *Tyrannosaurus rex* was famous as the biggest predatory land creature of all time. But the past few years have seen discoveries of even bigger meat-eating or carnivorous dinosaurs.

Fossils of *Giganotosaurus*, 'southern giant reptile', were uncovered in 1993 in Patagonia, Argentina. This huge hunter was slightly bigger than *T rex*, at more than 13 metres long and weighing over 6 tonnes. *Giganotosaurus* lived earlier than *T rex*, about 95–90 million years ago.

Fossils of *Spinosaurus* were first found in Egypt in 1912. This predator lived 100–95 million years ago, and had long, bony rods sticking up from its back that may have held up a 'sail' of skin. The original remains suggested a big predator, but not as big as *T rex*. However recent finds indicate that *Spinosaurus* may have been larger, maybe 16 metres long and 7 tonnes in weight.

QUIZ

Put these dinosaurs in order of size, biggest to smallest:
Tyrannosaurus rex   Deinonychus
Brachiosaurus   Spinosaurus
Compsognathus   Giganotosaurus

Answers:
Brachiosaurus, Spinosaurus,
Giganotosaurus, Tyrannosaurus rex,
Deinonychus, Compsognathus

Carcharodontosaurus, 'shark tooth lizard', was another massive hunter from North Africa. It was first named in 1931 and lived 100–95 million years ago. Recent discoveries in Morocco and Niger show that it could have been about the same size as T rex.

Another T rex-sized dinosaur was Mapusaurus, which lived in Argentina around the same time as T rex lived in North America. It was not as heavily built as T rex, weighing about 3 tonnes.

▼ This skull of Carcharodontosaurus measures more than 1.7 metres in length, with teeth 20 centimetres long. The human skull just in front of it gives an idea of just how big this dinosaur was.

▶ T rex and the other meat eaters were not the biggest dinosaurs by far. Much larger are huge plant eaters such as Brachiosaurus and Argentinosaurus.

INDEX

Entries in **bold** refer to main subject entries.

A

Acanthostega 16, 33
Age of Dinosaurs **50–51**, 57, 60, 64
Albertosaurus **65**, 112, **113**
Allodesmus 41
Allosaurus 64, **65**,111
ammonites 13
amphibians 16, 17, 18, 20, 33
Anancus 36, 37
anatomy **94–95**, 118
Anatosaurus 69
Andrewsarchus 31, 93
Anomalocaris 10, 11
Apatosaurus 50, **59**, 61, 63
Aphaneramma 17
Archaeopteryx 25, 33, 117
Argentavis 42
Argentinosaurus **60**
armadillos 45
armoured dinosaurs 51, **72–73**
arms 95, **100**, 113
Arsinoitherium 31
Arthropleura 16
arthropods 12, 16
Aviatyrannis 108

B

baby dinosaurs 75, **76–77**, **106**
Barosaurus 50, 60, **61**
Baryonyx **59**, 62
birds 13, 25, 33, 42, 50, 69, 80, 81, 117
bite strength, T rex 99, 102, 105
bone-head dinosaurs 84
brain, T rex 97
Branchiosaurus 20, 60, **61**, 75, 91
Brontotherium 30, 51
Brown, Barnum 114, 115

C

camels 39
Carcharodontosaurus 125

carnivorous dinosaurs 50, 51, 90, 93, 124
see also meat-eating dinosaurs
Carnotaurus **65**
cave bear 41
cave lion 8, 9
Charnia 11
Chasmatosaurus 23
claws 58, **62–63**, 65, 83, 84, 85
Climatius 14
Coelophysis **71**
cold-blooded animals 117
Compsognathus **83**, 111
Confuciusornis 25
Cooksonia 11
Cope, Edward Drinker 114
coprolites **103**, 116
Corythosaurus **67**
creodonts 29
Cretaceous Period 51, 91
crocodiles 22, 50, 52, 54, 57, 81, 87
Cynognathus 23

D

Daphoenodon 34
Daspletosaurus **113**
deer 39
Deinocheirus **62**
Deinonychus 51, **62**, 91, 111
Diatryma 80
Diictodon 19
Dilong 110
Dimetrodon 22, 50, **52**, 53
Dinictis 40
Dinohyus 34
Diplodocus 60, **61**, 77, 94
duck-billed dinosaurs 67, 69
Dunkleosteus 15

E

ears 66, 67
Edmontosaurus **58**, 59, 102, 103
eggs **74–75**, 76, 77, 85, 116, 117

Elasmosaurus 26
elephants 29, 31, **36–37**
entelodonts 34
Eogyrinus 17
Eoraptor 54, 55
Eotyrannus 108
Erythrosuchus 50, **52**
Euoplocephalus 72, **73**
Eusthenopteron 15
evolution 52, **56**, 69, 81
extinction **80–81**, 90
eyes 66, 67, 96,97

F

feathers 69, 110
feet **101**
fish 13, **14–15**, 27
food **102–103**
footprints 60, 61, 85, 101, 116
fossil experts 94, 118
fossils 10, 21, 25, 27, 30, **32–33**, 35, 58, **84–85**, 86, 87, **116**
Frithiof, Ron 'Tinker' 122
fur 23, 25

G

Gerrothorax 16
giant sloth 45
Giganotosaurus 64, **65**,124
Glyptodon 45
Gorgosaurus **112**
growth **106**
Guanlong 110

H

hadrosaurs 69, 74, 76, 102
Hatcher, John Bell 114
Hemicyclaspis 14
Hendrickson, Sue 120
herbivorous dinosaurs 50, 51, 91
see also plant-eating dinosaurs
herds 103
Herrerasaurus **54–55**
Hesperocyon 40, **81**
Heterodontosaurus 50
horned dinosaurs 72, 73

horses 28, 29, 38, 42, 44
humans 32, 41
hunting 91, 102, **104**, 124
Hylonomus 19
Hypsilophodon **62**
Hyracotherium 38, **81**

I

ice ages **8–9**, 36, 41
Ichthyornis 69
ichthyosaurs **68**, 69, 80
Ichthyostega 17
Iguanodon **63**, 71, 83
insects 11, 12, 16, 33
intelligence, T rex 97

J

'Jane' 123
Janenschia 50
jawless fish 14
jellyfish 11
Jobaria 50
joints 119
Jurassic Period 50, 108

K

'Kid Rex' 122

L

Lakes, Arthur 114
legs **54–55**, 70, 71, 94, **101**, 119
Leptictidium 28
lizards 50, 54, 81
lobefin fish 15, 17
Lystrosaurus 21

M

Macrauchenia 44
Maiasaura **76–77**
Mamenchisaurus 60, **61**
mammals 13, 25, **28–29**, 31, 50, 51, 53, 79, **80–81**, 93, 117
hoofed **38–39**
meat-eating **34–35**, 41
mammoths 9, 36, 37, 36, 51
Mapusaurus 125
marsupials 41, 42, 43
Mastodonsaurus 20, 21

126

ACKNOWLEDGEMENTS

All artworks are from the Miles Kelly Artwork Bank

The publishers would like to thank the following sources
for the use of their photographs:

t = top, b = bottom, l = left, r = right, c = centre

Alamy Page 88 Photos 12

Burpee Museum of Natural History Page 123 Jane: Courtesy of Burpee
Museum of Natural History

Corbis Page 98(b) Corbis; 114 Bettman; 115 Bettman; 117 Layne Kennedy;
118 DK Limited; 122 Louie Psihoyos; 124 Louie Psihoyos

Dreamstime Page 87 Mirkamoksha

iStockphoto.com Page 13 iStockphoto.com; 84 Joe McDaniel

Photolibrary Page 98(t) Robert Clark; 108 Salvatore Vasapolli;
121 Steve Vider

Reuters Page 120 Ho Old

Science Photo Library Page 119 Volker Steger

All other photographs are from: Corel, digitalSTOCK,
digitalvision, ImageState, iStockphoto.com, John Foxx,
PhotoAlto, PhotoDisc, PhotoEssentials, PhotoPro, Stockbyte

Every effort has been made to acknowledge the source and
copyright holder of each picture. Miles Kelly Publishing apologises
for any unintentional errors or omissions.